wedding cake
art and design

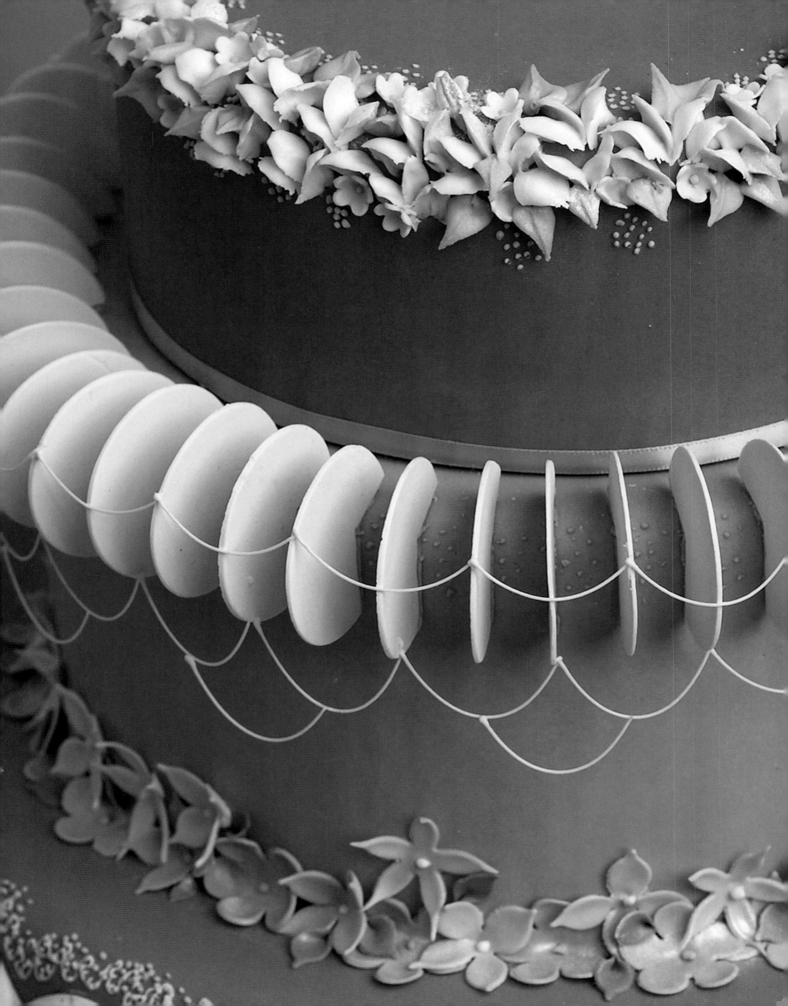

wedding cake art and design

A PROFESSIONAL APPROACH

Toba Garrett

Photography by Lucy Schaeffer

Illustrations by Christine Mathews

WILEY

JOHN WILEY & SONS, INC.

Published by John Wiley & Sons, Inc., Hoboken, New Jersey

Published simultaneously in Canada

For general information on our other products and services or for technical support,
please contact our Customer Care Department within the United States at (800) 762–
2974, outside the United States at (317) 572–3993 or fax (317) 572–4002.

Wiley also publishes its books in a variety of electronic formats. Some content
that appears in print may not be available in electronic books. For more
information about Wiley products, visit our web site at www.wiley.com.

Library of Congress Cataloging-in-Publication Data:

Garrett, Toba.
    Wedding cake art and design : a professional approach / Toba Garrett.
        p. cm.
    Includes index.
    ISBN 978-0-470-38133-5   (cloth)
    1. Cake decorating. 2. Wedding cakes. I. Title.
    TX771.2.G3634 2010
    641.8'6539--dc22

                                        2009052124

Printed in China

10 9 8 7 6 5 4 3 2

contents

for Chicquetta and Estelle

ACKNOWLEDGMENTS

Without the generous help and support of the following people, this book could not have been written. I owe them all a great deal of thanks and sincere gratitude. They are: Christine McKnight, Jorge Amaral, Jacqueline Beach, Michael Olivo, and Jeff Faust of John Wiley & Sons, copyeditor Chris Benton, and Alison Lew and Gary Philo of Vertigo Design. I also want to thank Rachel Livsey, who was my first editor and who greatly guided the inception of this book.

I would also like to thank Lucy Schaeffer, my photographer, Christine Mathews, my illustrator, Shane Walsh, Lucy's assistant, Scott Horne, prop stylist, and Ashley Norton, his assistant. I would also like to thank the reviewers of this book, Vincent Donatelli and Condra Easley.

Special thanks for the support from my husband and partner, James Garrett and all my family members who have shaped and guided me throughout the many years. To our beloved son Phoenix, we love and miss you. To my beloved sister Chicquetta and Aunt Estelle — you will always be in my heart. To my brother Kartrell, his wife Tess, my niece Kathleen, my sister Valerie, and my beloved parents — you are my source of inspiration.

And last, but not least, I would like to thank my good friend and agent Wendy Lipkind.

CHAPTER ONE

designing the cake

Designing and creating a wedding cake is an exciting opportunity. It is challenging, intimidating, a little scary, and, in most cases, an expensive undertaking. It is also a task that requires a great deal of skill, a lot of planning, and much patience. A wedding cake is uniquely personal because it is based on a couple's specific ideas. The design can be simple yet elegant and not require a lot of work; or it can involve many hours of labor, including intensive piping, sculpting, shaping, coloring, and structuring.

DESIGNING THE CAKE WITH THE COUPLE

The elements to consider when designing a cake in consultation with a bridal couple include color, texture, theme, shape, and décor.

The color scheme of the cake can be anything from a simple palette of pastel tones to something bold or complex, like reds, blacks, violets, and dark greens. The texture of the cake can be smooth (rolled fondant) or textural (such as "embossed rolled icing" inlay or appliqué or piping on a cake). The theme can be dramatic, whimsical, traditional, seasonal, or elegant. The shape can be traditional round or square, oval, horseshoe, or teardrop. The final design can incorporate a wide range of techniques, including simple to advanced piping, sugar flowers, marzipan sculpture, latticework, painting, advanced embroidery, and airbrushing. All of this will be based on the couple's budget, tastes, and expectations and the talent of the cake artist.

Let's look more closely at each of these tools used in the successful designing of a cake.

color

The color of the cake is perhaps its most important feature. Getting the color wrong when the bride has her heart set on something very specific can ruin the wedding celebration for the couple. The bride and groom often come to their appointment with a cake artist with a general idea of what they want the cake to look like and, most specifically, the color of the cake. Some couples may even bring in color swatches, a color wheel, or paint chips to make sure the cake artist knows what they want.

Color is used to set a mood. It expresses emotion, and it is essential to the overall ambience of the event. No longer are all wedding cakes white. Some couples may opt for subtle shades of white, such as off-white, ivory, cream, tan, or beige. Some couples may select pastel shades, such as peach, lemon yellow, soft pink, lavender, or sky blue, that will complement the wedding. And then there are couples who want bold colors, such as red, black, deep violet, dark blue, and burgundy. All of these colors are achievable, either by purchasing already-colored rolled icing fondants or by coloring your own white rolled fondant. Colored rolled fondant is more expensive

than white rolled fondant that you then color yourself. Also, coloring fondant yourself gives you flexibility in choosing and matching just the right color and tone. Practicing mixing colors with small amounts of white fondant can prevent the more costly mistake of ending up with the wrong color mixed into a large amount of white fondant.

You can use a color wheel or an online color schemer to review complementary color tones. An online color schemer is a color studio that provides you with hundreds of color tones and palettes. You select a color, and it provides you with complementary or harmony color tones. It's a super visual color wheel. Several good online color schemers to try are www.colorschemer.com and www.colorspire.com. This kind

of wheel can be especially useful when the couple is seeking colors that complement the base color of the cake.

MIXING COLORS

Mixing colors is an art all to itself. Looking at a color swatch or wheel is one thing; creating that color in icing is another. Food colors come in liquid, paste, gel, and powdered forms. Gel colors are the most economical, being less expensive and easier to blend into icing. To create and test colors, use a small amount of icing and carefully color the icing using a toothpick. Note approximately how much color is needed to color a small amount of icing and then use that proportion

to calculate what you need to color a much larger portion.

Another technique is to squeeze a tiny portion of food color into an artist tray and then add a tiny amount of gel or paste labeled "bright white" or "liquid whitener" to bring out the pastel tone of the color. Bright white and liquid whitener are titanium dioxide and are more liquid than regular gel colors. Care should be taken not to use too much of this, as food colors (especially these whiteners) contain glycerin. This ingredient is used to keep colors soft, and too much of it will change the consistency of the icing and the drying time. Once you mix your colors using these whiteners you can get an immediate color tone, which spares you a lot of guesswork.

USING LIQUID WHITENER

You can add powdered food color to a gel color to get more intensity, but only after the liquid whitener has been added to the gel color. Adding powdered food color to gel or paste colors without the liquid whitener will have no effect.

texture

A huge variety of textures can be used on wedding cakes. A textured wedding cake is not traditional, but it can offer the bridal couple a fun, exciting, and different perspective. A smooth cake can be painted to look textural, or a textured rolling pin can be rolled over icing to give a fabriclike look to a cake. This is especially useful when a bride-to-be wants the texture of her wedding gown matched in icing. A textured rolling pin that matches or comes close to the designs on a bridal gown can

probably be found. For those designs where there are no special rolling pins, you will have to use ingenuity, such as piping the textured design directly on the cake or creating a silicone mold using a piece of the lace from the bridal dress. With a mold, all you need to do is press icing into the mold; when the icing is released, it will have the exact same lace impression as the bride's dress.

Fabric ribbon or icing ribbons can also be used to give texture to a cake. Or the cake can be draped in rolled icing, which imparts a

spectacular texture. Piping Swiss dots all over a cake also adds a beautiful texture, and overpiping gives it a dramatic three-dimensional look.

All of these ideas and many others must be at your fingertips when you interview a couple to design their special cake. But always keep the budget in mind—the more intricate the cake, the more expensive it will be!

theme

Theme wedding cakes are all the rage. Couples are very imaginative when it comes to creating cake concepts that represent their lives. Sometimes the most outrageous concepts for a cake can bring a smile even to the most creative cake artists.

A theme can be anything. A couple may want blown-up balloons on the wedding cake or the cake itself shaped into a hot-air balloon; a cake decorated with marzipan farm animals; a wedding cake made of cupcakes or decorated with cookies; a cake that looks like the sea or a beach scene with pebbles and seashells and sand, all made out of sugar; a cake decorated with snack foods; a cake shaped like the pyramids; or a patriotic-themed cake with flags. The possibilities are endless. A theme cake does not have to be gimmicky; it also can be

breathtakingly beautiful using classical or creative design work. It can be artistic, rustic, modern, or traditional. Almost anything can be designed and turned into a wedding cake.

These types of cakes can require a lot of planning, sculpting, food painting, and hand-shaped ornaments made out of a sugar material. Theme cakes can also be more expensive than traditional cakes, as many techniques are needed to create a couple's dream. As the cake artist, you would be

wise to limit the scope of the design based on the couple's budget. Ultimately, you want a good working relationship with the couple, and the couple has the final say as to what the cake should look like. But it's important to inform the couple that the cake will be created in the spirit of the design chosen. Except for anything major, you should have artistic license to make small changes without notifying the couple, as long as those changes are done in the spirit of the agreed-on design.

shape

Cakes in general can come in any conceivable shape. Wedding cakes for the most part are still predominantly round, square, oval, heart-shaped, and scalloped around the edges, but that doesn't mean that a couple will actually choose one of these shapes. A couple may wish for a wedding cake shaped like a horseshoe or a pyramid, a ball shape or a kidney shape, or even a cake shaped like a mountain. There is no end to the possibilities

the couple may come up with, and a skilled cake artist can create a wide range of different-shaped cakes.

There are many things to consider when choosing a nontraditional shape: choosing a sturdy cake, using preserves instead of a mousse or curd filling, and creating strong structural support. Also, when icing an unusual shape, you should have extra icing to allow for a much larger circumference, especially when icing a cake in rolled icing.

You also need to consider how the cake will be cut and served when the shape is unusual. You might need to make the unusual shapes larger to accommodate the bride and groom's reception, or you can have an iced sheet cake in the kitchen of the reception hall to help accommodate the guests.

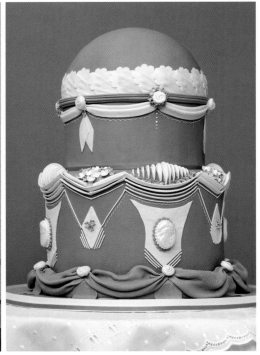

décor

The design of the cake is the most important reason a prospective bride and groom come to a cake artist. Each cake artist has a body of work in a specific style. That style is the artist's trademark. A prudent cake artist can move easily into any style and thus give the bride and groom a wide range of design options. At the cake artist's fingertips are a wide range of techniques, including textured rolling pins, premade sugar flowers, simple to advanced piping, inlay work, appliqué, airbrushing, marzipan sculpting, chocolate modeling, gumpaste designs, pastillage, painting, and perhaps pulled or blown sugarwork. The techniques for these and other decorative elements are covered in detail in subsequent chapters.

The design of the cake determines how expensive the cake will be, so the couple's budget will determine how elaborate the cake design can be. The more techniques used to design the cake, the more the cake will cost. A wise cake artist will produce several drawings based on the couple's price range, thus giving the clients the best possible options for their special day.

For example, the cake artist draws three drawings: a high-end drawing, a moderately priced drawing, and a low-end drawing. The high-end drawing might contain several sprays of hand-shaped flowers and fine pipework, like brush embroidery or fine freehand embroidery piping. A moderately priced drawing might have one large spray of sugar flowers on the top tier and a gilded monogram of the couple on the middle tier. A low-end drawing might have purchased premade gumpaste flowers, a simple bead border on all the tiers, and perhaps some Swiss dots.

THE CONSUMER BRIDE

Bridal couples invest a wealth of planning in their wedding, from selecting a wedding gown, finding a floral designer, and selecting a reception hall to finding the perfect cake artist. Before choosing the cake artist who will produce their dream wedding cake, the bride and groom have some homework to do.

First, they should set a price range for what they are willing to pay for their wedding cake, noting that very popular or celebrated cake artists will cost considerably more than someone perhaps not as well known or well publicized. This doesn't mean that a couple can't get the cake of their dreams—there are talented cake designers all over, charging a wide range of prices. The cost of the cake can vary from area to area and from state to state. There are no general or specific prices for wedding cakes from a cake artist. Cost is determined by how large the cake will be (how many guests it is to serve) and the intricacy of

the design. Prices can range from $5.00 to $15.00 per serving, and the cost can go much higher, depending on the intricacy of the design and the popularity of the cake artist. If a couple is not prepared to pay these kinds of prices, another option is getting a wedding cake as a package deal through the couple's caterer, which can cost from $2.50 to $8.00 per serving. The last option would be to purchase a wedding cake from their local bakery. The price may be lower, but the couple will be limited with regard to designs, icings, and fillings. The small details that a cake artist can add to a cake may not be possible at a local bakery.

When first contacted by the couple, you can help them come prepared for your first meeting by telling them what you will need to know. Being prepared means knowing the guest count for the reception, the colors they want incorporated into the design—including swatches or other types of color samples—the overall theme they want represented, and their

budget. They should know the number of tiers they want, should have an idea of what type of cake they desire, including fillings, and, if they want the cake artist to match a design from the bride's dress to the cake, they should bring a picture of the dress to their consultation. They should also be aware of any site considerations, such as stairs and the size of the reception room. Last, they should bring a checkbook.

Almost every cake artist now has a website, which gives the prospective bride and groom an opportunity to see the designer's portfolio. If you do not have a website, you will most certainly have a photo portfolio to share with a couple during their appointment.

The couple will generally meet with you at least once, and often several times, before signing a contract. The following is the typical sequence of steps involved in choosing a wedding cake, describing both your role and that of the consumer.

step one

First contact. The bridal couple calls the cake artist and asks for an appointment. When the clients call, they likely already have a gut feeling about the cake artist. Often the purpose of this appointment is for the clients to talk to the cake artist and perhaps see some of his or her work more closely and to inquire about prices. This also gives the cake artist an opportunity to observe the client and determine whether this opportunity will likely lead to a congenial transaction or one that will be exceptionally stressful. At the conclusion of this appointment, the clients indicate that they will get back to the cake artist after reviewing all of their options. This gives the clients the opportunity to visit with other cake artists and compare designs and prices. The cake artist then makes notes about the clients, their demeanor or enthusiasm, and their ability to pay.

step two

Sampling flavors. The clients call back and indicate they are strongly leaning in the cake artist's direction. The cake artist can set up another appointment with the clients—perhaps this time with a few samples of cakes, icings, and fillings. This step can be done at the very first meeting as well if the cake artist feels strongly that the clients are leaning his or her way.

Having samples ready when the clients come in is a way of extending a good first impression and goes a long way toward helping the artist secure the job. The cake artist might wish to limit the types and flavors of cakes and icings at this stage unless the artist is part of a large establishment that produces a wide variety of cakes on a daily basis.

CLIENT CONSULTATIONS

Clients can meet with a cake artist several times before a decision is made. The first step is the introduction, with the client seeing some cakes and perhaps a portfolio. The second step is a paid consultation, which can include sampling cakes and icings and a quick sketch of the cake to be considered. The next step would be for the clients to secure the artist's services for the established wedding date. At this stage, the cake artist may ask for a one-third deposit on the total cost of the cake. Normally the contract would be signed at the same time as a deposit is made. The last step would be to get the balance of the payment two weeks before the cake is due. All of this can change depending on the cake artist and the clients. All of these steps can be reduced to just two steps or, in a rare case, just one! The cake is then produced three to five days before it is delivered.

step three

step four

First sketches. This second (or third) meeting with the clients generally becomes a paid consultation. This means the clients pay a fee for the cake artist's time. As a means of securing the contract from the client, the cake artist would be wise to tell the clients that this fee is deducted from the total cost of the cake should they wish to sign a contract. Generally, a consultation fee can be from $50 to $150. At this meeting the clients continue to look through books or pictures of cakes designed by the cake artist. They also bring in pictures and ideas of their own. During this meeting the cake artist begins sketching an idea

of what the client is looking for. This does not have to be a perfect drawing but should give the clients an idea of what the cake would look like. If the cake artist does not draw, software is available to help design a cake. Once the cake is designed and the couple has decided on the type of cake flavor, icing, and filling, the process is almost finished.

It is possible that the clients still won't commit to the cake designer, even after they have paid a consultation fee. The fee should still be applied, even if the client decides months later to order from the cake artist.

Deposit and contract. The final step, once the clients have chosen the cake artist as their designer, is for the cake artist to request a deposit from the clients and for both to sign a contract. The deposit is typically one-third of the total cost of the cake. This deposit should be received within two weeks of the consultation date (Step 3) to secure a date for the wedding cake. This is another tactical move to secure the contract, but the cake artist should take care not to overwhelm the client. Once the contract is signed, the cake artist should request full payment two weeks prior to the wedding day.

DESIGN TECHNOLOGY

Cake artists and bridal couples alike can use a software program called Wedding Cake Design Pro to help them design the couple's dream cake. This 3-D tool helps everyone visualize the perfect cake by programming the software for specifics such as cake shape, the number of tiers, the type of cake designs that can be used on the side or top of the cake, what type of border piping to use at the bottom of each tier, and what types of elements the bride and groom wish to have on the top of the cake. The site is weddingcakedesignpro.com. The software can be ordered and downloaded immediately.

CAKE SIZE AND COST

The size of the cake is determined by the number of reception guests. For instance, a cake that feeds 150 people, with each person getting a standard 1 × 2-in. (2.5 × 5.1 cm) serving, can be composed of 6 × 4-in. (15.2 × 10.2 cm), 10 × 4-in. (25.4 × 10.2 cm), and 14 × 4-in. (35.6 × 10.2 cm) layers. At $10 per serving, this cake will cost $1,500. This price would be considered average for a cake prepared by a noted cake artist. (For more information on serving cakes of all shapes and sizes, see pages 257–266.)

The techniques required to decorate a cake will also affect the cost. For example, to reduce the cost of a cake, a couple may choose a fresh floral arrangement on the top tier instead of handmade sugar flowers. In this case, the cake artist would need access to a floral artist that produces organically grown flowers and, of course, flowers that are nonpoisonous. When fresh flowers are used, the cake artist and floral artist should determine far in advance of the wedding date who will place the flowers on top of the wedding cake.

Another option that can reduce the cost of a cake is to prepare the cake layers in Styrofoam. Styrofoam is often used as a cake dummy in photography. When used in place of an actual wedding cake, a small section of the Styrofoam is cut away and a section of actual cake is put in its place. Or the top tier of the cake is real and the bottom two tiers are Styrofoam. To feed the guests at the reception hall, sheet cakes are cut and served to the guests.

FLAVOR COMBINATIONS

The flavor of the cake is of utmost importance. Wedding cake flavors can range from a simple butter cake to lemon, almond, walnut, genoise, red velvet, chocolate, pound, fruit, or even a decorated cheesecake. Flavor combinations are important to the palate, and the wedding cake should complement any other desserts served at the reception. For example, vanilla and almond are a wonderful flavor blend, as are lemon and raspberry, chocolate and raspberry, lemon and coconut, peach and vanilla, lemon and almond, and many more. The cake artist should experiment with flavor combinations and test-market them to get good feedback. Ultimately, the clients will determine what they want, but it's up to the cake artist to steer the clients in the right direction. (See the Flavor Combinations chart, page 236.)

ESTIMATING TIME

The time it takes to prepare the cake varies depending on the intricacy of the cake and the human resources available. A cake designer with no staff might limit the number of cakes produced per year, versus a larger establishment with several employees that can produce several cakes a month or even a weekend. For the individual cake artist, estimating the time it will take to produce the cake will vary depending on the techniques used to decorate the cake. For example, a three-tier cake to serve 150 people can be done within a few days and even less if several people work on it. If the cake design is relatively simple—the cake enrobed in rolled fondant, Swiss dots on all three tiers, a bead border around the bottom of each tier, and perhaps a large spray of sugar flowers (made in advance or purchased ready-made) on the top tier—the cake can be done easily within one or two days. A more intricate design with five tiers, brush embroidery or freehand embroidery on all five tiers, bead piping around the bottom of each tier, classical drapery work, and several sprays of gumpaste flowers can take upward of three to five days to complete, provided the flowers were done in advance.

For a typical cake, the layers can be baked two to three days in advance, cooled, wrapped well in plastic wrap, and then refrigerated. The filling can be made the same day as the cake or on another day. Most cake artists use a commercial filling to save time and cost.

The icing is generally made a day or two in advance. Generally, if a cake is enrobed in rolled fondant, there is a layer of buttercream icing under the rolled fondant. This helps adhere the fondant to the cake and it gives the cake a richer, more delicious taste. The rolled fondant is generally purchased rather than made from scratch in order to save valuable time.

Any sugar floral work can be done way in advance as it does not spoil or require refrigeration.

TRANSPORTATION AND ASSEMBLY

Transporting and assembling a cake is not as difficult as it might seem. The design of the cake determines this issue. The majority of cakes seen in bridal magazines are stack tiered, which means that one tier sits on top of another, with dowel rods inserted into each tier for support. Stacked three-tier cakes travel quite easily. However, the more tiers there are, the greater the risk. If the tiers are elevated with pillars, then the assembly would need to be completed at the wedding reception site.

Most cakes can be transported quite easily in an SUV, van, or station wagon with a flat surface. Rubber foam can be placed on the flat surface to minimize shock during travel. The cake should be in a box with the bottom lined with nonskid material. This will ensure that the cake, which is attached to a cake board, will not move.

In the case of a stacked six- to eight-tier cake, the cake artist can stack the bottom three tiers and place them in a box. Then the next three tiers can be stacked and placed in a separate box, and the last two tiers can be stacked and placed in a separate box. All three boxes of stacked cakes can be assembled at the reception hall.

Depending where you live, delivery services are available specifically for cakes. In the New York area, there is a service called Signature Delivery. You contact the service and explain what is to be delivered. The service provides large vehicles and caring individuals who will pick up your cake and carefully deliver it to the reception hall. You can ask to go with the deliverer to ensure that the cake arrives safely. This service will pick up and deliver almost anywhere.

TRANSPORTING CAKES BY PLANE

If traveling by plane, the cake artist should contact his or her local carrier and inquire about regulations for shipping a cake by plane. If this is a small two-tier cake, it might just fit under the seat in front of you if someone is traveling with the cake. If it's three tiers or higher, ask if the flight attendant can place the cake in the front of the plane. This should be requested in advance of the flight. If the cake artist can build a platform on which to place the tier cakes and wrap the cake and the platform in heavy plastic wrap, the cake can travel in the belly of the plane. Again, the cake artist would need to make these arrangements with the carrier in advance, and someone on the other end of the flight would need to retrieve the cake when it arrives.

creative designs

Leaf texture, monogramming, ribbon loops, and classic floral designs are featured in the stately cakes in this chapter. Each cake is unique, yet they are all tied together with classic white, lilac, mint green, and dark green foliage. These creative combinations make the cakes in this chapter designs you will admire again and again.

the couple

Ronda and Allen are looking for that perfect wedding cake. Ronda is a legal secretary. She collects porcelain dolls, and she is taking calligraphy classes. Allen manages a shoe store. For relaxation he enjoys gardening. They visited several websites and spoke to a couple of local cake designers before choosing one in their area. The color scheme for their wedding is white, mint green, and lilac. The couple is looking for a cake that serves 100 people. They would consider an even smaller cake to cut cost, with perhaps a half-sheet cake to accompany the wedding cake.

the consultation

The cake artist presents a portfolio and books on wedding cakes. As the couple browses through the books, the cake artist takes out a notebook and jots down different designs of cakes the couple has an interest in. The cake artist then takes out a sketch pad and begins to sketch rough designs based on the variety of ideas the couple is leaning toward.

elements of the cake

The couple would like a pound cake with a lemon filling. The cake artist suggests a Lemon Pound Cake with a Lemon Curd filling. The cake artist also suggests an Italian buttercream icing to sandwich and coat the tiers before they are enrobed in Rolled Fondant flavored with lemon extract. The first cake's tier sizes are 6, 8, and 10 inches (15.2, 20.3, and 25.4 cm), which would serve up to 110 slices. The second cake's tiers are 6, 8, and 9 inches (15.2, 20.3, and 22.9 cm), which would serve up to 100 guests. The third drawing has tiers of 6 and 9 inches (15.2 and 22.9 cm) and serves only 75 slices.

development of the cake designs

The cake artist uses the sketches to come up with creative designs for the couple. The following three cakes represent the cake artist's creativity during the development process:

CAKE 1: *The Textured Rose Cake* The first sketch is somewhat traditional but has a creative edge. The cake is a three-tier white cake with hand-shaped sugar roses on top with dark green leaves. The cake artist is thinking about some type of texture on the icing and possibly a monogram but isn't sure at the initial stage of this drawing. The cake artist wants to reflect Allen's and Ronda's interests in calligraphy and gardening in the cake designs by choosing a decorative monogram and traditional floral design.

CAKE 2: *The Textured Ribbon and Rosebud Cake* The cake artist draws a three-tier cake, with a green icing in mind. The cake artist is thinking of piped leaf sprays on the tiers, lilac-colored rosebuds, and a monogrammed plaque with some sugar ribbons.

CAKE 3: *The Two-Tone Ribbon and Textured Leaf Spray Cake* In this design, the top tier is white and the bottom tier is lilac. The cake artist sketches cornelli lace piping and an arrangement of blossoms, buds, and sugar ribbons.

The couple is dazzled by the sketches but can't decide which design to ask the cake artist to develop at this time. They want some time to think about all three sketches.

cake 1

THE TEXTURED ROSE CAKE

This three-tier cake is enrobed in white rolled fondant with a foliage texture design on the top and bottom tiers. The middle tier is untextured and is adorned with scalloped oval plaques with the couple's shared initial. The plaque is decorated with cornelli lace and lilac buds.

The top tier is adorned with clusters of hand-shaped white roses dusted with pearl luster, and deep green foliage accents the cake. The cake drum is also textured, and the finale is a small floral arrangement on the side of the middle tier.

how-to techniques

CLASSIC ROSE

Shape about ¼ oz (7 g) of gumpaste into a round ball and then into a cone. Make a hook at the end of a piece of 22- or 24-gauge white or green florist wire covered in florist tape. Dip the end of the hook into egg whites and then ease it into the large end of the cone to a depth of about ½ in. (1.3 cm). Secure the paste to the wire by pinching it. Let dry for at least several hours or overnight.

Rub a tiny amount of white vegetable shortening on the work surface. With a nonstick rolling pin, roll out about 2 oz (57 g) of the remaining gumpaste until you can see through it. Carefully pick up the paste and put it on a clean area of the work surface that is sprinkled lightly with cornstarch. Cut out four petals using a metal or plastic rose petal cutter. Place the cutouts on a cell pad and lightly soften the edges with a ball or dog-bone tool. Keep the other petals covered with plastic wrap to prevent them from drying.

Pick up the rose base and lightly brush it with egg white. Pick up one of the petals, holding it in one hand with the wire base in your other hand. Bring the petal

bottom one-third of the distance from the top of the petal and press it to the base. Tuck the left side of the petal to the base and overlap the right side of the petal, leaving a tiny opening at the top. Slightly

pull the right side back with your thumb for a nice detail.

Brush the first petal and base lightly with egg white. Place the second petal over the seam of the first and slightly higher. Before

Clockwise from the bottom right: Creating a wired base and petals, adding petals to create a rosebud and a half rose, and adding final petals to complete the classic rose.

attaching the next petal, brush the right side of the second petal about one-third of the distance, if right-handed. If left-handed, brush the left side of the second petal. Attach the third petal to the brushed side of the second, overlapping by about one-third. Brush the third petal with egg white one-third of the distance to the right of the petal, if right-handed. Attach the fourth petal to the newly brushed side, with the right side inside the second petal and overlapping it. This is a rosebud.

With the same cutter, cut five more petals. Soften the edge of each petal and cover with plastic wrap to prevent drying.

Lightly brush the sides of the rosebud with egg white. Attach a fifth petal to the seam of any of the overlapped petals. This petal should be slightly taller than or the same size as the previous petals. Brush and overlap each of the remaining four petals. Once all are attached, pinch the center of each petal for roselike detailing. This is a half-rose. Let this dry for 24 hours before attaching the final petals.

For the last five petals, choose the rose petal cutter that is one size larger than the cutter used for the first nine petals.

GLUING GUMPASTE FLOWERS

Gumpaste flowers can be glued with several mediums: fresh egg whites, pasteurized egg whites, or gum glue (a mixture of 6 parts water to 1 part gum arabic), and even, in a pinch, just plain water. Water holds, but not as well as the egg whites or gum glue. Since gumpaste flowers are not eaten as a rule, fresh egg whites may be best because they are generally available and easiest to obtain. However, when securing pieces of fondant to a cake that is to be eaten, the cake artist should use pasteurized egg whites or water.

Roll out the paste and cut five more petals, softening each with a ball or dogbone tool. Because of their large size, you need to let these petals dry slightly before attaching them to the half-rose. Lightly brush the half-rose base with egg white. Attach each petal as you did the last five of the half-rose. They should be the same height as or slightly taller than the previous petals.

NOTE: For an even larger rose, cut seven additional petals with the same cutter and attach them as you did to the last five petals. The petals should be the same height as or slightly taller than the previous petals.

To complete the rose, roll out about ½ oz (14 g) leaf-green gumpaste. Cut out the calyx with a medium-size calyx cutter. Ease the calyx onto the wire first and then brush each sepal with egg white and ease the calyx onto the back of the rose. Put a small pea-sized bit of green paste on the back of the calyx and shape it onto the wire to complete the rose.

To color the white rose, brush pearl luster on the petals for a luminous look.

ROSE LEAVES

Roll 1/2 oz (14 g) of deep green gumpaste into a ball. Shape the ball into a log about 3 in. (7.6 cm) long. Rub the work surface with a tiny amount of white vegetable shortening and place the log on it. With a nonstick rolling pin, press the center of the length of the log, rocking the pin back and forth to flatten the log. Roll the paste from the center to one side, preferably toward yourself. Roll it petal thin at one side of the center and gradually thicken it on the other side. The center should be no thicker than 1/8 in. (3 mm).

Dust a clean area of the work surface with a light coating of cornstarch. Place the flattened strip of gumpaste on the cornstarch. Cut out leaf shapes with a rose leaf cutter, positioning the cutter so the base of the leaf is on the thick part of the strip and the tip is on the thin part. Cut as many leaves as possible and place them under plastic wrap.

Repeat this technique until you have about 2 dozen leaves.

To wire-cut leaves, dip the tip of a 28-gauge wire into egg white and insert it into the thick part of the leaf to about 1/4 in. (6 mm) deep. Repeat until all the leaves are wired.

Place each leaf in a silicone leaf press and firmly press the top and bottom presses to give it texture. Soften each leaf by placing it on a cell pad and applying light to medium pressure with the dogbone tool around the edges.

For a natural look to these dark green leaves, pass each leaf over steam from a teakettle. This creates condensation and gives a waxy look to the leaf. Let each leaf dry overnight.

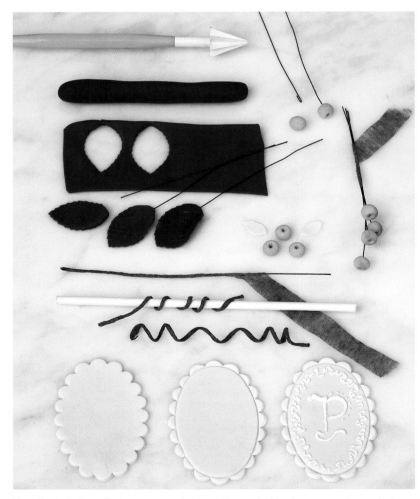

From top to bottom: Rolling a gumpaste log, cutting and wiring leaves, creating and wiring lilac buds, creating spiral foliage, and cutting and piping on a monogrammed plaque.

SCALLOPED-EDGE OVAL PLAQUE AND MONOGRAM

Color about 3 oz (85 g) of mint-green gumpaste. Rub the work surface with a tiny amount of white vegetable shortening and place the gumpaste on it. With a nonstick rolling pin, roll out the paste to about ⅛ in. (3 mm) thick.

Dust a clean area of the work surface with a light coating of cornstarch. Place the flattened gumpaste on the cornstarch. Cut out four scalloped oval plaques with a scalloped cutter (see Templates, page 240). Before the plaques dry, place a plain oval plaque cutter over the scalloped-edge plaque and press it into the plaque. The plain oval plaque cutter should be ¼ in. (6 mm) smaller than the scalloped plaque cutter. Let the plaques dry overnight.

Transfer the monogram onto a dry plaque (see Templates, page 240). Trace the pattern on a piece of transparent paper. Reverse the pattern and trace the opposite side of the pattern.

Place the traced pattern right-side up on the scalloped oval plaque. Tape the pattern securely with masking tape. Carefully trace the pattern once more with a #2 graphite pencil. Press firmly as you make a carbon copy of the reverse side of the pattern. Once the pattern is retraced, carefully remove the masking tape. Repeat this for the next three oval plaques.

Using a #2 round tip in a small paper cone filled with Meringue Powder Royal Icing, carefully pipe the monogram. Let dry for several hours. Pipe cornelli lace around the monogram with a #0 round tip.

To pipe cornelli lace, the tip should slightly drag the surface at a 45° angle. Move the tip in one continuous loose curve (see page 109).

LILAC BUDS

For unwired buds, take a pea-sized amount of lilac gumpaste and rotate it into a round ball. Press the serrated side of the cone and serrated tool in the center of the bud. This leaves a textured throat to the center of the bud.

To wire the buds, dip an unhooked edge of a 28-gauge wire into egg white and stick it halfway inside the small ball of paste. Pinch the spot where the wire is inserted to secure it. Let dry for several hours.

To finish the lilac buds, dust the center of the buds with lilac petal dust.

SPIRAL FOLIAGE

Take a long piece of 28-gauge green wire and tape it carefully with florist tape. Wrap the taped wire on a long dowel. Remove the taped wire to reveal the spiral foliage.

TEXTURED ROLLED FONDANT

Measure out 1 lb (16 oz or 454 g) of white rolled fondant. Knead the fondant with a little solid vegetable shortening until pliable. Shape the fondant into a disk. Dust the surface lightly with cornstarch and roll out the fondant to about ¼ in. (6 mm) thick with a rolling pin. Roll the textured rolling pin onto the fondant to reveal the texture on the pin.

Rolling a textured pin onto fondant, from bottom to top.

THE TEXTURED RIBBON AND ROSEBUD CAKE

This is a three-tier cake, enrobed in mint-green rolled fondant. The top tier is adorned with a large scalloped oval plaque with his initial, her initial, and their shared initial on the plaque. The monogram is gilded and decorated with lilac buds and hand-shaped rose petals. The back of the oval plaque is decorated with large textured ribbons (from the same textured rolling pin used in the first cake design) and lilac rosebuds, other buds, and rose petals. Sugar ribbons also extend from the front of the plaque down to the second tier of the cake.

The second tier has foliage piping that matches the textured rolling pin in white, and there is a small spray of rosebuds on the fondant-covered cake drum next to the bottom tier.

how-to techniques

LILAC ROSEBUDS

See Classic Rose, page 20. Follow the instructions up to the rosebud stage. Complete the rosebud with a calyx. Dust the center of the rosebud and the edge of each petal with lilac petal dust.

TEXTURED RIBBONS

Measure out 4 oz (114 g) of white gumpaste. Knead the paste with a little white vegetable shortening until pliable. Rub the work surface with a tiny amount of white vegetable shortening and roll out the paste about ¼ in. (6 mm) thick. Roll the textured rolling pin over the gumpaste until the paste is

⅛ in. (3 mm) thick. Cut out strips of ribbon using a ruler and an X-acto knife. The ribbons should be 2 in. (5.1 cm) wide and 7 in. (17.8 cm) long. Score the edges of the ribbon strip with a quilting wheel to give a "stitch" effect. Let strips dry for 15 minutes. Then glue both ends together with egg whites, forming a loop. Turn the loop on its edge and let dry overnight.

Bottom: A flat piece of textured gumpaste shaped into a loop. Top: Cutting a plaque and using a clay gun to create a textured rope border.

GILDED MONOGRAMMED PLAQUE

Roll out green gumpaste following the instructions for the Textured Rose Cake (see page 19) and cut out a large scalloped plaque. Emboss the inside of the plaque with a plain round oval cutter that is ¼ in. (6 mm) smaller than the scalloped plaque. Let dry thoroughly. Transfer the monogram onto the plaque as was done in the Textured Rose Cake. Outline the monogram with a #2 round tip and Meringue Powder Royal Icing. Let dry for several hours.

To gild the monogram, mix ¼ tsp of gold powder with a few drops of lemon extract. Paint the monogram with a #1 sable paintbrush dipped into the gold mixture.

Finish decorating the plaque with a textured rope border using a clay gun and lilac rose petals and blossoms.

PIPED LEAF SPRAY

Transfer the piped leaf spray onto the cake with a stickpin or pipe it freehand. To transfer with a stickpin, trace the pattern onto a piece of transparent paper. Place the traced pattern on the cake and carefully secure with masking tape or stickpins. Transfer the pattern to the cake by outlining it with a stickpin. Be sure the pinpricks are close together to reveal a good likeness of the pattern. Remove the pattern from the cake. Pipe over the pinprick pattern with a #0 tip and Meringue Powder Royal Icing.

Top to bottom: Piping an oval-shaped leaf with piped lines inside the shape; a completed piped leaf spray.

cake 3

THE TWO-TONE RIBBON AND TEXTURED LEAF SPRAY CAKE

This is a two-tier cake enrobed in rolled fondant. The top tier is white, while the bottom tier is lilac colored. Cornelli lace in a scalloped piped design adorns the bottom tier and a spray of two-toned sugar ribbons, along with five-petal blossoms, buds, leaf blades, and a textured leaf spray (which resembles the texture on the first cake design) sits on top of the bottom tier. Both tiers sit on a fondant-covered drum that matches the color of the bottom tier, and the tiers are contrasted with green and lilac fabric ribbons.

how-to techniques

TWO-TONE RIBBONS

Roll out 2 oz (57 g) of green gumpaste and 2 oz (57 g) of white gumpaste on a work surface rubbed with a tiny amount of white vegetable shortening. The paste should be $^1/_8$ in. (3 mm) thick. Sandwich one strip on top of the other and reroll the paste until it is between $^1/_{16}$ and $^1/_8$ in. (1.5 mm and 3 mm) thick. Cut out strips about $^1/_2$ in. (1.3 cm) wide and 5 in. (12.7 cm) long. Score the very edge of each strip with a quilting wheel.

Shape a 24-gauge florist wire into a U. Insert the U into the gumpaste strip to a depth of about $^1/_4$ in. (6 mm). Brush a little egg white over the wire to secure it and then bend the strip over into a closed U shape.

Top, from left to right: The steps for blending two colored gumpaste strips to create one strip. Bottom, left to right: Shaping and wiring the strip for two-toned ribbons.

LEAF SPRAY

Rub a work surface with a tiny amount of white vegetable shortening and roll out 2 oz (57 g) of white gumpaste into a log. Cut out leaves with a cutter (as for the Textured Rose Cake, see page 22), or cut out oval shapes freehand. Wire the leaves and then score five lines in each leaf (using the opposite end of a quilting wheel). Allow each leaf to dry and then petal-dust each leaf with pearl luster.

Arrange three leaves together into a spray and place a small pea-sized piece of white gumpaste in the middle of the leaf spray, attached with egg whites or a little royal icing (see illustration).

FIVE-PETAL PULLED BLOSSOM

Form a pea-sized piece of lilac gumpaste into a round ball. Place the ball in the palm of your non-writing hand and use the middle finger of your writing hand to shape one end into a cone. Dip a modeling stick into cornstarch and place it in the large part of the paste, about ⅛ in. (3 mm) deep. Cut five

slits, equally spaced, around the paste about ¼ in. (6 mm) deep. Remove the modeling stick and pinch each petal, sticking your index finger under each petal and flattening the top of the petal with your thumb. Use your thumb to round off the petals. Make a cavity in the center of the flower using a modeling stick. Make a hook in the end of a 28-gauge wire, dip the wire

in a little egg white, and wipe off any excess. Thread the wire through the flower from the unhooked end. When the hook reaches the center cavity, turn the trumpet end of the flower as you ease the hook through the flower. Pinch the trumpet lightly to attach the wire to the flower. Petal dust the edges of the petals with lilac petal dust and the center cavity with moss green petal dust.

Bottom and left: Creating and wiring lilac buds and taping the buds into a spray. Right: Creating wired gumpaste leaves and taping them into a leaf spray. Center: The finished leaf spray.

LEAF BLADES

Color 2 oz (57 g) gumpaste a dark leaf green and wrap in plastic wrap. Remove ¼ oz (7 g) green paste and shape it into a round ball. Rub a tiny amount of white vegetable shortening on the work surface. Place the ball on the work surface and use a nonstick rolling pin to roll it into a log about 3 in. (7.6 cm) long.

Brush a little egg white on a 24-gauge green or white florist wire and insert the wire into the log of gumpaste to a depth of about ½ in. (1.3 cm). Pinch the end of the paste to secure it to the wire.

Rub a tiny amount of white vegetable shortening on the work surface and place the wired gumpaste on it. Press a nonstick rolling pin in the center of the paste to flatten it slightly. Thin the left and right sides of the paste with a modeling stick, leaving a ridge in the center. Part of the center ridge contains the inserted wire. With a modeling stick, thin the ridge above the inserted wire.

Return the wired paste to the work surface and place the end of the wire at the 12 o'clock position. Position an X-acto knife at the end of the paste to the left of the wire at a 45° angle. Drag the knife across the paste, making an oval shape from the back to the front. Stop the curve at the 6 o'clock position. Reposition the knife at a 45° angle at the end of the paste to the right of the wire. Drag the knife, making a curve that meets the left curve at the center point of the leaf. Remove the excess paste and lift the leaf from the wire.

From bottom to top: Rolling a gumpaste log, flattening, cutting, and shaping into a leaf blade.

Place the leaf on a cell pad with the wire at the 12 o'clock position. Position a veining tool (the opposite end of a quilting wheel) at a 45° angle starting at the center of the leaf's base. Drag the veiner with medium pressure from the base to the tip of the leaf. Then position the veiner about ½ in. (1.3 cm) to the left of the center vein. Drag the tool to make another vein, this time at a slight angle, from the base to the tip of the leaf. Score another vein to the left of the center vein. Now score two veins to the right of the center vein.

Let dry for several hours or overnight. When completely dried, pass the leaf blades over steam from a kettle to create condensation. This gives a natural shiny look to the leaves. Let dry overnight. The leaf blade is complete.

SCALLOP DESIGN WITH CORNELLI LACE

Measure the circumference of the bottom tier with a piece of parchment paper. Fold the measured parchment paper in half. Draw a scallop pattern, starting about 1 in. (2.5 cm) high from the left end of the paper. Draw scallop curves, 2 in. (5 cm) in length from the left of the pattern to the tip of the right edge.

Cut the pattern with a pair of scissors. Then place the pattern against the cake and pinprick the pattern on the cake with stickpins.

Pipe a scallop design over the stickpin pattern with a #2 round tip and Meringue Powder Royal Icing. Let dry and then pipe over the #2 round tip pattern with a #0 round tip and dark green royal icing. Pipe a cornelli lace pattern on the inside edge of the piped scallops.

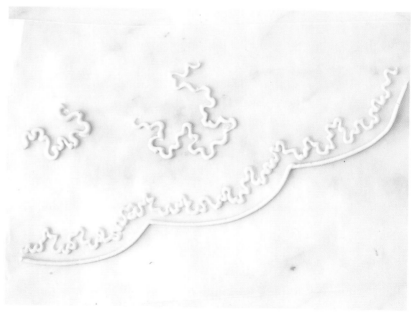

From top to bottom: Freehand cornelli lace and cornelli lace in a scalloped design.

CHAPTER THREE

romantic designs

Simplicity, beautiful floral work, and delicate piping are the hallmarks of romantic wedding cake designs. The cake artist draws on the couple's romance and passion when coming up with these unique cake designs. The flooded butterflies, sandwiched heart shapes, and flooded bells featured in these cakes are all symbols of love and romance.

cake 1

FLOODED BUTTERFLY AND CLOSED TULIP CAKE

This beautiful three-tier cake is iced in lemon/egg-yellow rolled fondant. There are Swiss dots on the top and bottom tiers of the cake, and two flooded butterflies drift near the top tier. On the middle tier sits a lavish display of closed tulips in white and yellow, sprays of forget-me-nots, variegated ivies, and dark-colored foliage. All of this sits on a fondant-covered drum, which is adorned with peach pearls and hand-shaped blossoms.

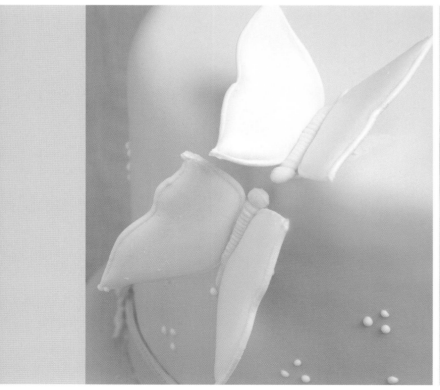 

how-to techniques

FLOODED BUTTERFLIES

First, trace the pattern for the flooded butterflies (see page 245). Place it on a flat surface and tape the ends. Then cover the flat surface with a piece of plastic wrap or wax paper and secure it tightly.

Fill a small paper cone with a #2 round tip and 1 oz (28 g) of Egg White Royal Icing. This will be used to outline the butterflies. Next, fill a medium-size paper cone or a small squeeze bottle with 2 oz (57 g) of Flood Icing. This will be used to create the butterflies.

Position the tip at a 45° angle to the pattern and trace it with the tip just barely above the surface. To fill in the outline, position the squeeze bottle or cornet with the Flood Icing in the center of the design. Apply light pressure and allow the icing to flow into the outline. The icing should not spread more than ½ in. (1.3 cm) from the perimeter of the design. Stop and remove the cone. With a toothpick, move the icing to the outline. Work quickly, because the icing sets quickly. Allow 2 to 4 hours or overnight for the butterflies to dry. To remove the butterflies, carefully run an offset metal spatula under the butterflies to release the icing from the plastic wrap. Attach with Egg White Royal Icing to the surface of the cake. This flooding technique can be used to create any other simple shapes as well.

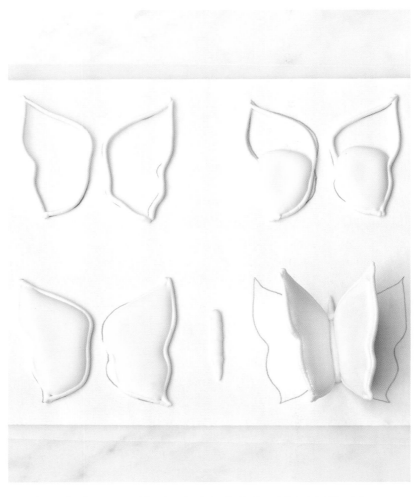

Top, left to right: Outlining and flooding the butterfly. Bottom, left to right: The full flooded and final assembled flooded butterfly.

CLOSED TULIPS

To make the base, shape ¼ oz (7 g) of gumpaste into a cone like that for a rose. Dip a hooked 24-gauge wire in egg white and ease it into the bottom of the paste. Secure the bottom of the paste to the wire and let dry for 30 minutes. Score three equal lines around the cone from bottom to tip with a veining tool or a rounded toothpick. The scored base is a tulip bud, or you can use the scores as a guide for placing tulip petals. Make several buds and let dry for several hours or overnight.

For the petals, select a tulip pattern or cutter, if available. Closed tulips can be made in an oval shape or have a scalloped top with rounded edges and a shaped bottom. To create the petals, rub a tiny amount of white vegetable shortening on the work surface and use a nonstick rolling pin to roll out some of the white or yellow paste. Place a pattern over the paste and cut out six petals or transfer the paste to a work surface with a light coating of cornstarch and cut out six petals. Cover the petals with plastic wrap until ready to use.

Add texture to each petal by firmly pressing it in a tulip press.

You can soften the edges of the petals with a dogbone tool if you like.

Brush a dried tulip bud with egg white and place the first petal at a seam. The petal should be at least ½ in. (1.3 cm) taller than the tip of the bud. Secure the petal to the base and use the base to shape the

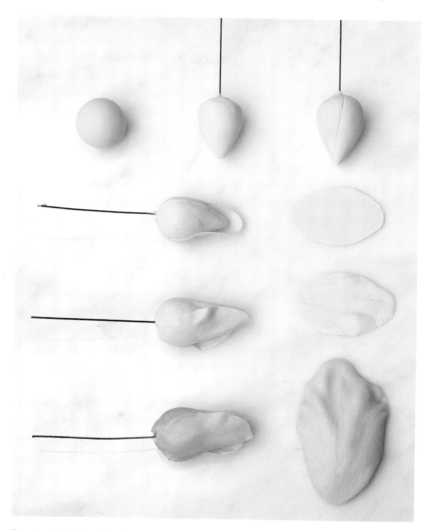

From top to bottom: Creating a wired base, adding the first three petals, and adding the final three petals at the seam of the first three to complete the closed tulip.

bottom of the tulip. Lightly cup the tip of the petal forward. Overlap the second petal about one-third of the distance of the first petal. Attach the second petal with a little egg white. Repeat with the third petal, making sure it fits inside the first petal. Let dry for 30 minutes.

To attach the last three petals, lightly brush the tulip with egg white and attach the first petal at an overlapped seam. Attach the next petal with egg white one-third of the distance of the previous petal. Follow this with the last petal, making sure to tuck it inside the fourth. Shape the top of each petal and allow the flower to dry thoroughly.

When the tulip is dry, brush it with daffodil-yellow petal dust, starting at the bottom and allowing the color to fade toward the top. Brush the edge of each petal with yellow or orange petal dust. Finally, brush green petal dust at the bottom of the flower, allowing the color to fade as it is brushed upward.

MERINGUE POWDER VS. EGG WHITE ROYAL ICING

Meringue Powder Royal Icing is used frequently in the book and by many cake artists. It's used so often because it is safe and free from salmonella. In fact, royal icing made with meringue powder tastes better because most meringue powder contains sugar, vanilla, egg white solids, edible gums, alum, and salt.

Most pipework can be done successfully with Meringue Powder Royal Icing. However, when the occasion calls for fine stringwork, trellis work, or any fragile, freestanding lace pieces, the cake artist must use an icing made with the strongest alum available. Egg White Royal Icing can be made with pasteurized egg whites, but the results are not quite the same. Stringwork piped using pasteurized egg whites has tiny holes and doesn't look nearly as elegant as royal icing made with fresh egg whites, and the freestanding pieces aren't as strong. For many, there is no problem with Egg White Royal Icing, but the cake artist should advise the bride and groom of their options.

FORGET-ME-NOTS

The technique for the five-petal forget-me-not is the same as that for the five-petal basic pulled blossom. Divide 2 oz (57 g) gumpaste in half. Color the halves with different shades of bluish violet gel food color, one lighter than the other. Wrap both halves in plastic wrap to prevent drying.

To make the flower, form a pea-sized bit of bluish violet gumpaste into a round ball. Shape one end of the ball into a cone. Dip a modeling stick into cornstarch and place it in the large part of the paste. Cut five slits, equally spaced, around the paste. Follow the same procedures for making the five-petal flower (see instructions for the Textured Ribbon and Rosebud Cake, page 31). Wire the completed flower and allow it to dry. Make more flowers using the other shade of bluish violet paste. Create the bud with the same technique as for the basic five-petal pulled blossom bud (see instructions for the Textured Ribbon and Rosebud Cake, page 31). Allow to dry. Drying time can be as little as 2 hours.

To petal-dust the flower, brush a deeper shade of violet or purple petal dust on each petal, but do not completely cover them. Brush the trumpet of each forget-me-not with a deeper shade of petal dust.

Mix a small amount of lemon-yellow gel food color with a little liquid whitener. Brush the inside of some of the flowers with the yellow color, leaving the center unpainted. Using untinted liquid whitener, brush the inside of the remaining flowers, leaving the center unpainted.

For the bud, brush the bottom with a deeper shade of purple. You may also paint the bud's center with a yellow gel color and liquid whitener mixture or with untinted liquid whitener.

Top: Rolling, shaping, and wiring forget-me-nots; a finished spray of forget-me-nots. Bottom: Shaping, wiring, and finishing a variegated ivy leaf spray.

SWISS DOTS

Load a small paper cone with 1 Tbsp (14 g) of meringue powder flood icing, which is Meringue Powder Royal Icing softened to the consistency of sour cream with water or egg whites.

Snip the paper cone with a pair of scissors and hold the tip at a 90° angle to the sides of the cake. Apply light pressure and allow a small ball of icing to flow from the tip of the paper cone. Keep the tip stationary as you build up the ball of icing. Stop the pressure and re-move the tip of the cone from the ball of icing. The icing will drop back and settle to make the surface of the ball completely smooth.

IVY LEAVES

Roll ½ oz (14 g) white gumpaste into a ball. Shape the ball into a log about 3 in. (7.6 cm) long. Rub the work surface with a tiny amount of white vegetable shortening and place the log on it. Follow the same procedure used for leaves in the Textured Rose Cake (see page 19).

Cut out ivy leaves with a cutter, positioning the cutters so the base of the leaf is on the thick part of the strip and the tip on the thin part. Cut as many leaves as pos-sible and place them under plastic wrap.

Follow the same procedure for inserting the wires, embossing, and softening the leaves as used in the Textured Rose Cake (see page 19). Petal-dust the flower with mustard yellow/orange. You can leave the very edge of the flower undusted. Then brush a little moss-green petal dust from the base and up through the center, over the mustard yellow/orange.

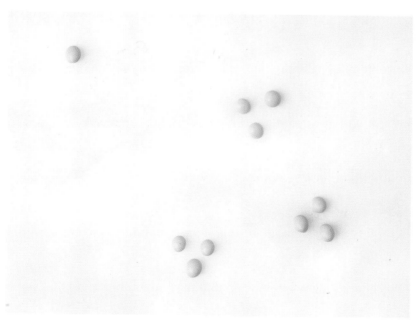

From left to right: Piping Swiss dots.

cake 2

FLOODED BELL, CALLA LILY, AND BLUE TULLE CAKE

This is a two-and-a-half-tier cake. The very top tier is a "half-cake" turned on its side. All two and a half tiers are iced in white rolled fondant. Flooded bells adorn the half-cake on top, with Bouvardia (Australian wildflowers) and strings of blue sugar ribbons cascading from the top tier. On the very top of the half cake is a beautiful spray of calla lilies, blue tulle with Swiss dots piped on it, and a lovely spray of Bouvardia and foliage.

Bouvardia embroidery is piped delicately on the middle tier, and the bottom tier pulls it all together with blue tulle tied around the entire tier with Swiss dots piped directly on the tulle. A small Bouvardia spray is nestled in front where the tulle comes to a bow. This is an intimate cake for a romantic couple.

how-to techniques

ARUM OR CALLA LILY

For the spadix (base) of the flower, measure out ¼ oz (7 g) yellow paste and shape it into a 2-in. (5.1 cm) cylinder or elongated cone. Dip ¼ in. (6 mm) of 24-gauge wire into egg white and ease the wire into the pointed end of the cone to a depth of about ½ in. (1.3 cm). Pinch the end of the paste to secure it to the wire. Make several more bases and allow them to dry for several hours or overnight.

For a pollen effect, dip the spadix in egg white and coat it with cornmeal mixed with yellow petal dust (for a deeper color). Let dry for 2 hours.

For the spathe (petal) of the flower, rub a tiny amount of white vegetable shortening into the work surface and use a nonstick rolling pin to roll out 1 oz (28 g) of white gumpaste until it is petal thin. Place this on a work surface dusted lightly with cornstarch. Cut out a petal with a metal or plastic cutter. Press a flower former or corn husk onto the petal to form lines. Place the petal on a cell pad and soften the edges with a ball or dogbone tool.

To assemble, brush the bottom of the petal with a little egg white and place the cone at the bottom center. The bottom of the cone should be just inside the petal's edge. Overlap the right side of the petal over the cone. Brush a little egg white on the overlapped side and overlap the left side of the petal over the right. Slightly open the petal and fold the sides back for a more natural shape.

To color the lily, brush daffodil-yellow petal dust in the center of the flower, slightly under the spadix and extending up toward the tip. The color should fade out ½ to 1 in. (1.3 to 2.5 cm) before the top edge. Brush yellow petal dust around the flower's trumpet and back. Then brush moss-green petal dust over the same area and blend the green color with the yellow petal dust.

Rolling a spadix and coating with cornmeal.

Texturing a petal with a cornhusk.

Left to right: Partially covering the yellow center with a textured petal; the complete arum or calla lily.

BOUVARDIA

This is a four-petal Australian wildflower. It is white and waxy, and the only color is a little moss-green petal dust at the bottom of the trumpet.

Measure ½ oz (14 g) gumpaste, remove a pea-sized bit, and cover the balance of the paste in plastic wrap. Position the pea-sized piece of paste in the palm of your non-writing hand. Place the middle finger of your writing hand on top of the paste and rotate until a rounded ball forms. Shape the paste at one end of the ball to form a cone.

Dip the pointed end of a modeling stick in cornstarch and insert it in the large end of the cone to a depth of about ⅛ in. (3 mm). Cut four slits into the rounded end of the paste, about ¼ in. (6 mm) deep. Remove the stick and open the florets.

Just as you did for the five-petal blossom (see page 31), shape the florets by placing your thumb under one of them and your index finger on top, or vice versa. Press the paste lightly to flatten it and then turn your thumb and index finger to the left and right sides of the petal. Lightly pinch the petal on the side, then pinch the petal at the tip, pulling lightly, to form the shape of the petal. Do the same to the three remaining florets.

Make a small cavity in the center of the flower with the modeling stick. Make a hook in the end of a 28-gauge wire, dip the wire in a little egg white, and wipe off any excess. Thread the wire through the flower from the unhooked end.

When the hook reaches the center cavity, turn the trumpet end of the flower as you ease the hook through the flower. Pinch the trumpet lightly to attach the wire to the flower. Stick the wired flower into a piece of Styrofoam to dry. Drying time can be as little as 2 hours.

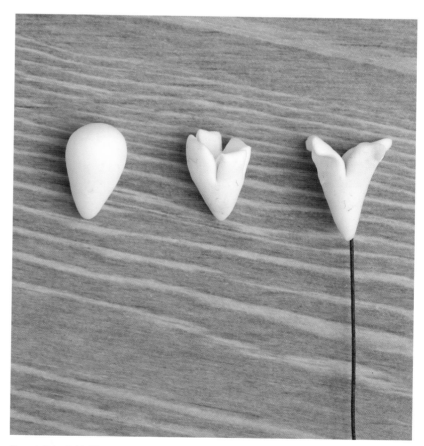

From left to right: Shaping the gumpaste, cutting four slits into the base, and hand-shaping and wiring to form a Bouvardia flower.

BUDS

Measure a pea-sized amount of gumpaste and rotate it into a round ball. Dip the unhooked end of a 28-gauge wire into egg white and stick it halfway inside the small ball of paste. Pinch the spot where the wire is inserted to secure it. Using your thumb and index finger, pinch the top center of the paste. Slightly pull the pinch out to form an onion shape. Stick the wired bud into a piece of Styrofoam to dry.

To petal-dust the four-petal blossom, brush a little moss-green petal dust on the trumpet part of the flower. For the bud, brush the moss-green petal dust underneath and up to the middle. Both flower and bud are complete.

FLOODED BELLS

First, trace the pattern for the flooded bell (see page 246). Place it on a flat surface and tape the ends. Then cover the flat surface with a piece of plastic wrap or wax paper and secure it tightly.

Fill a small paper cone with a #2 round tip and 1 oz (28 g) of Egg White Royal Icing. This will be used to outline the bells. Next, fill a medium-size paper cone or a small squeeze bottle with 2 oz (57 g) of Flood Icing. This will be used to create the bells. Position the tip at a 45° angle to the pattern and trace it with the tip just barely above the surface. To fill in the outline, position the squeeze bottle or corner with the Flood Icing in the center of the design. Apply light pressure and allow the icing to flow into the outline. The icing should not spread more than 1/2 in (1.3 cm) from the perimeter of the design. Stop and remove the cone. With a toothpick move the icing to the outline. Work quickly, because the icing sets quickly. Allow 2 to 4 hours or overnight for the flooded bells to dry. When dried, carefully run an offset metal spatula under the flooded piece to release the icing from the plastic wrap. Attach with Egg White Royal Icing to the surface of the cake.

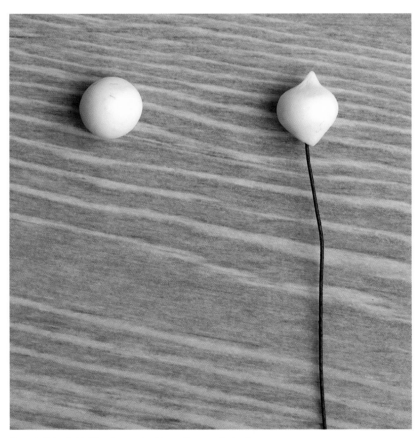

From left to right: Shaping and wiring a Bouvardia bud.

BOUVARDIA EMBROIDERY PIPING

Fill a small paper cone with a PME #0 tip and 1 Tbsp (14 g) of Meringue Powder Royal Icing. Position the tip at the surface of the cake. Apply a small burst of pressure, forming a small ball, and then ease off the pressure as you pull the tip to form a point at the end of the ball. Pipe three more exactly the same, forming a small cluster. Then drag the tip to the surface to form a small curve. Pipe tiny stems off the main curve and pipe groupings of 3 dots at intervals alongside the stem to form the embroidery.

Clockwise from top left: The steps for piping Bouvardia embroidery.

SWISS DOTS ON TULLE

Measure ½ oz (14 g) of Flood Icing into a small paper cone, with a #0 metal tip, or use a paper cone with the tip snipped off and no piping tip. Pipe dots randomly over the tulle.

From left to right: Gathered tulle and piping tiny dots of Royal Icing onto the tulle to create Swiss dots.

cake 3

HEART-SHAPED CAKE WITH
FLOODED HEARTS AND CARNATIONS

This is a dramatic two-tier heart-shaped cake, iced in peach rolled fondant. Sitting upright on the top tier is a cut-out heart-shaped sugar plaque from pastillage. The sugar plaque is decorated and adorned with yellow and peach carnations and green foliage. Heart-shaped piping adorns the sides of the top tier, and the top and bottom tiers are adorned with cornelli lace near the shoulder of each tier.

Flooded heart shapes, attached to fabric ribbons, cascade from the top tier and also on the back of the bottom tier.

how-to techniques

PASTILLAGE HEART SHAPE

Dust a work surface with a light coating of cornstarch and roll out 3 oz (85 g) of Pastillage. Rub a tiny amount of white vegetable shortening onto the work surface and use a nonstick rolling pin to roll out the paste to a thickness of $1/16$ to $1/8$ in. (1.5 to 3 mm) thick. Dust a clean area of the work surface with a light coating of cornstarch, transfer the paste to it, and cut out the shape with a large heart-shaped cutter. Let dry overnight. The next day, sand the edges and surface with fine sandpaper. Decorate the plaque with plunger flowers and embroidery piping.

CARNATIONS

Measure out 4 oz (114 g) of gum-paste. Color half of the paste a lemon yellow and the other half peach. Wrap the paste in plastic wrap to prevent drying.

To make the carnation bases, roll a pea-sized amount of paste into a tiny ball. Dip the end of a 24-gauge white or green wire in egg white and ease the ball onto the wire. Place your thumb and middle finger on the wired ball of paste and rotate it back and forth, applying pressure at the end of the paste to secure it to the wire. The completed base should look like a cotton swab and be no longer than

$1/4$ to $1/2$ in. (6 mm to 1.3 cm). Make several bases.

Choose carnation cutters or rounded scalloped cookie cutters $1^1/2$ to 2 in. (3.8 to 5.1 cm) in size.

Rub a work surface with a tiny amount of white vegetable shortening and use a nonstick rolling pin to roll out the colored or neutral paste until it is petal thin. Transfer the paste to a work surface dusted with a light coating of cornstarch. Cut out three petals with the carnation or cookie cutter and cover two of them with plastic wrap. Place the third petal on a little cornstarch and cut little slits in each of the scallops, about $1/4$ in. (6 mm) deep.

From left to right: Creating a scalloped petal with a wired base, ruffling the petal, folding in half, and overlapping one side to the center to form a partial carnation.

Place ½ in. (1.3 cm) of a rounded toothpick on the petal. Use your index or middle finger to rotate the toothpick back and forth to ruffle the petal. Do this on each of the scallops. Ruffle the other two petals and cover them again with plastic to keep them moist.

To assemble, brush the carnation base with egg white and ease the wire through the center of one of the petals. Sandwich the base in the center of the petal. Brush egg white up the petal's center and overlap the left side. Put a little egg white on the overlapped side and overlap the right side of the petal. Gently gather the petal, applying light pressure at the trumpet while carefully shaping the flower. This is the first floret.

Brush egg white under the first floret and ease the second petal onto it as you did the first. Sandwich the floret and overlap the petal. Gently gather the petal to make the floret fuller. Repeat with the third petal; however, reverse this petal so the ruffles are on the underside. Egg-wash, sandwich, and overlap the petal. Gently gather until the ruffles are full and lush. Use a toothpick to fluff the ruffles.

For a quick carnation calyx, roll out green paste petal thin and cut with a small or miniature rose calyx cutter. Ease the calyx onto the carnation. Brush the sepals with egg white and secure the calyx to the back of the carnation. Next, roll a tiny ball of green paste and ease it onto the wire. Secure it to the end of the calyx and pinch it to secure it to the wire.

To color the carnation, brush the center of the carnation with a deep shade. Carefully brush the same color over each ruffle.

From left to right: A partial carnation with one ruffled and folded petal, adding the second ruffled petal, and the complete carnation with the final ruffled petal added.

HEART-SHAPED PIPING

Fill a small cone with a PME #o tip and 1 Tbsp (14 g) of Meringue Powder Royal Icing. To form the heart shape, position the tip at the cake surface. Apply a small burst of pressure (as for the Bouvardia Embroidery Piping, page 51). Make a small ball and then ease off the ball and form a small line. Now squeeze another small ball and, this time, ease off the pressure and pull a small line next to the first line, forming a heart shape.

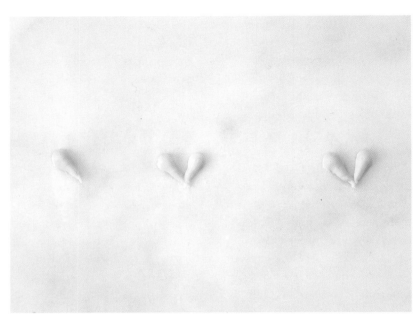

From left to right: Piping heart shapes.

FLOODED HEART SHAPES

Trace the patterns for heart shapes (see page 247). Outline heart shapes with a #2 round tip and Egg White Royal Icing. Fill a paper cone with 1 oz (28 g) of Flood Icing. Position the tip at a 45° angle to the pattern and trace it with the tip just barely above the surface. To fill in the outline, position the squeeze bottle or cornet with the Flood Icing in the center of the design. Apply light pressure and allow the icing to flow into the outline. The icing should not spread more than 1/2 in. (1.3 cm) from the perimeter of the design. Stop and remove the cone. With a toothpick move the icing to the outline. Work quickly, because the icing sets quickly. Allow 2 to 4 hours or overnight for the flooded pieces to dry.

When dried, release the flooded hearts from the plastic wrap. Turn one of the hearts over. Squeeze a little royal icing in the center of the heart. Then place a ribbon in the center of the heart, making sure the ribbon covers the royal icing, then squeeze a little more icing on top of the ribbon and sandwich another heart directly over the ribbon.

This flooding technique can be used to create any other simple shapes as well.

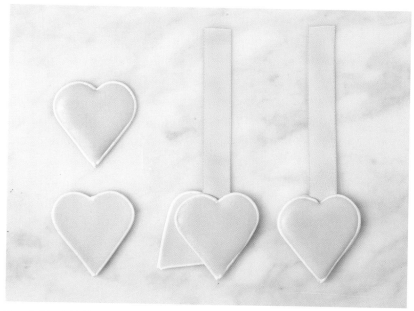

From left to right: The front and back of a flooded heart shape; both hearts sandwiched with a strip of ribbon.

CHAPTER FOUR

textured designs

Earth-tone colors in beige, mocha, brown, and ivory create the perfect backdrop for textured wedding cake designs. These cakes show beautiful texturing using satin stitching, brush embroidery, and textured rolling pins. By playing with different shapes, including squares, ovals, and round tiers, the cake artist can produce a range of distinctively different, beautiful cake designs.

the couple

Nathan and Margaret-Ann come from the North Carolina area and have decided to have a small fall wedding with 50 guests. This energetic couple is passionate about their love, and they both have an eye for details. Nathan is a freelance graphic designer. His parents own a fabric warehouse, and he co-manages the business for them. He enjoys biking and fishing. Margaret-Ann is a seventh-grade teacher who enjoys romantic novels and traveling, and she is a member of a quilting guild.

The couple chose a local caterer who includes the wedding cake as part of the catered event. The caterer showed them some simple wedding cake designs, but none caught their eye. The couple decided to hire a cake artist to create their cake. For their fall wedding, they are considering a beige, brown, off-white, and cream color palette.

the consultation

After looking through pictures and books and sampling cakes and icings, the couple can't decide on just one cake. So the cake artist makes some notes on the styles and techniques that the couple loved and then decides to do some quick sketches.

elements of the cake

The couple wants chocolate, chocolate, and more chocolate. The artist suggests a Dark Chocolate Fudge Cake with rich chocolate Ganache filling iced in Chocolate Buttercream Icing and enrobed in Chocolate Rolled Fondant. The first drawing has a $9 \times 7 \times 3$-in. ($22.9 \times 17.8 \times 7.6$ cm) rectangular top tier and an $11 \times 9 \times 3$-in. ($28 \times 22.9 \times 7.6$ cm) rectangular bottom tier. The cake serves 55 to 65 guests. The second drawing has 6-, 9-, and 12-in. (15.2, 22.9, and 30.5 cm) oval tiers that are 3 in. (7.6 cm) high and serves 75 to 85 guests. The third drawing includes 6- and 10-in. (15.2 and 25.4 cm) round tiers that are 4 in. (10.2 cm) high and serves 60 to 65 guests.

development of the cake designs

The cake artist uses the sketches to come up with three creative designs for the couple. All three cakes are designed to incorporate fabric, texture, stitching, and monograms to echo the couple's shared interests.

Cake 1: *Satin Stitch Monogrammed Cake* The cake artist quickly sketches a two-tier cake in a rectangular shape. The artist envisions ruffles in tones of mocha and beige and a beautiful monogram that would have his, her, and their shared initials.

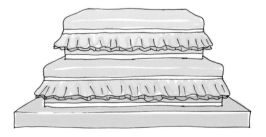

CAKE 2: *Brush Embroidery Cake* In this sketch, the cake artist draws a three-tier cake in an oval shape. The artist is considering a spray of fall gumpaste flowers or just a spray of fall foliage. The artist draws some floral work on the three tiers and is considering doing some brush embroidery work.

CAKE 3: *The Groom's Cake* The cake artist suggests a groom's cake to go along with the wedding cake. The couple seems excited by this idea. The cake artist asks for suggestions, but the couple cannot think of one. So the artist draws a two-tier round cake and draws a facsimile of a tuxedo, along with bow tie and boutonniere. The couple loves the idea but is still considering whether to have a groom's cake.

SATIN STITCH MONOGRAMMED CAKE

This design is a two-tier rectangular cake, enrobed in butter-scotch/mocha rolled fondant. The bottom tier is decorated in fondant double ruffles: the bottom ruffle is beige, and the top ruffle is a mocha color. The ruffles are attached at an angle and almost cover the shoulders of the rectangular cake. The top edge of the ruffles is finished with a piped rope design.

On the top tier, the cake is decorated in the same ruffle design as the bottom tier. On top of the cake is a large monogram of his, her, and their shared initials. The monograms are outlined and flooded with royal icing and then decorated with satin stitch. The stitchwork gives an exciting textured design to the cake that resembles fine linen. There is also a foliage design that runs through the monogram, and the cake is finished off with some gumpaste blossoms.

how-to techniques

MONOGRAM AND SATIN STITCH

First, trace the pattern (see page 248) on a piece of transparent paper. Then place the pattern on the cake. Carefully tape the edge of the pattern with masking tape. Using a stickpin, pinprick the entire monogram design, including all of the embroidery work, directly onto the cake. Carefully remove the pattern to reveal the pinprick outline. Or, as an alternative, turn the traced pattern over and trace

the opposite side of the pattern, then place the pattern right-side up and place it on a rectangular piece of gumpaste or pastillage plaque. Tape the pattern securely with masking tape. Carefully trace the pattern once more with a #2 graphite pencil. Press firmly, as you are making a carbon copy of the reverse side of the pattern. Once the pattern is retraced, carefully remove the masking tape (see sidebar).

To begin the outlining, place a #3 round tip and 1 Tbsp (14 g) of Egg

White Royal Icing in a small paper cone. Carefully outline the monogram. When outlining long lines of a pattern, remember to lift the tip and let the icing drop to the surface. Keep the tip to the surface when outlining curves and short lines.

Next, place a #0 round tip and 1 Tbsp (14 g) of Egg White Royal Icing in a small paper cone. Carefully pipe over the embroidery around the monogram, remembering to keep the tip close to the surface.

From left to right: A flooded monogram letter, beginning the satin stitching, and a completed satin-stitched monogram letter.

Next, place 2 oz (57 g) of Flood Icing in a medium-size paper cone without a tip. Cut the tip of the paper cone so the Flood Icing begins to flow from the cone. Position the tip of the cone inside the monogram and begin to carefully squeeze the bag. Allow some of the icing to build up inside the monogram. Using a toothpick, move the softened icing so it fills the monogram within the outline. Continue flooding until the monogram is complete. Let dry for 2 hours, or until the flooded monogram is dry to the touch.

When the monogram is dry, the satin stitching can begin. Position the cone with the #0 tip and Egg White Royal Icing at the upper left-hand corner of the monogram. Squeeze the bag as you drag the tip from left to right over the surface of the monogram. The lines should be extremely tight, with no spaces between them.

To stitch the embroidery around the monogram, position the #0 tip at one end of the embroidery and then move the tip back and forth, covering the embroidery in satin stitch.

When you satin-stitch a large monogram letter, you might wish to divide the large letter in half, that is, satin-stitch from the left edge of the letter to the middle of the letter and stitch from top to bottom. Let dry 15 minutes. Then satin-stitch from the middle of the letter (where the left side ends) to the right edge of the letter — from top to bottom.

PLACING MONOGRAMMING ON A SUGAR PLAQUE VS. DIRECTLY ON THE CAKE

Placing the monogram and satin stitch on a separate sugar plaque gives you more flexibility and more time to create a well-done design. When transferring the monogram directly to the cake, work quickly as the cake underneath is perishable. The plaque can be done in advance and placed directly on top of the cake and then removed before cutting and serving. Furthermore, the plaque can be saved as a keepsake of this special day and saved for many years.

Placing the monogram on a separate sugar plaque allows you to correct mistakes, which can be removed easily with a toothpick or a slightly damp cloth. For an added dimension, you can place the plaque at a 45° angle on the cake and prop it up with a spray of sugar flowers at the back of the plaque. This makes a stunning presentation and is a selling point to the couple.

RUFFLES

To make ruffles, lightly dust the work area with cornstarch and then roll out commercial fondant (with additional vegetable gum added to it) or gumpaste very thinly. Cut out a circle with a large fluted or scalloped cutter; then cut out the inner circle with a small round cutter.

Place the cut-out circle on cornstarch. Place a toothpick about ½ in. (1.3 cm) on the paste and apply pressure back and forth with one or two fingers. As the pressure is being applied, the paste begins to ruffle. Continue to ruffle the paste until you go around the complete circle. Then cut the circle and stretch out the paste. Turn the paste over and apply water lightly on the reverse side of the ruffle. Turn right-side up and attach to cake.

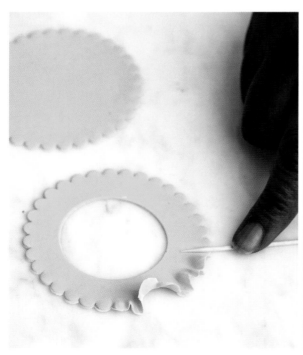

Using a rounded toothpick with a fair amount of pressure to ruffle a piece of gumpaste.

Completed piece of ruffled gumpaste.

PIPED ROPE BORDER

Fill a small paper cone with a #3 round tip and Meringue Powder Royal Icing. Position the metal tip where the rope border is to begin. The tip should be just slightly above the cake. Pipe a small, elongated S shape. Position the tip perpendicular to the center of the bottom curve. Apply pressure as you raise the tip slightly and pull the tip toward you. Now move the tip over the tail of the previous S curve as you create another elongated S curve.

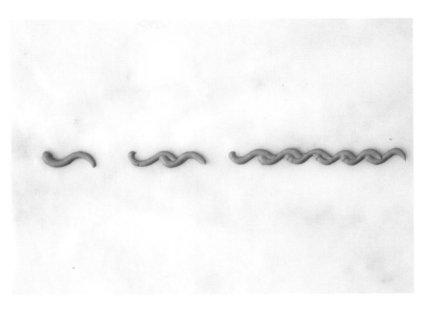

From left to right: Piping a rope border.

CUTTING AND PRESERVING A ROLLED FONDANT CAKE

Rolled fondant cakes don't cut as well as buttercream-iced cakes. Therefore, a good serrated bread knife is your best cutting tool. Always allow for additional servings. If a client has a reception for 50 guests, for example, you should provide a cake that serves 55 to 60 guests, but charge for only 50 guests. This gives the person cutting the cake some flexibility in case all of the servings are not exactly the same.

Reserving the top tier for the couple's first anniversary is not always assumed. The couple would need to request this, and the cake artist would need to make larger bottom tiers or a side tier to allow for it. Of course, the cake artist charges the couple for the uncut tier and arranges to provide a box with instructions for preserving the cake for one year.

To preserve it, the cake should be placed in a cake box and taped securely. Then the cake box is covered in aluminum foil, covered in plastic wrap, and placed in a freezer. To defrost, take from the freezer the night before the cake will be eaten and place in the refrigerator. In the morning, remove it from the refrigerator and place on a counter to defrost for several hours, still in the wrappings. Then unwrap. There is no guarantee that the cake will still look as nice as it was when first frozen and no guarantee of the taste.

cake 2

BRUSH EMBROIDERY CAKE

This dainty design is a three-tier oval cake enrobed in ivory rolled fondant. All three tiers of the cake are hand-brushed in the brush embroidery style, which gives a lifelike texture feeling to the cake. The pipework is an open rose with leaf foliage and is piped in a gold/mocha royal icing.

On the top tier is a spray of large foliage in beige, gold, and chocolate, accented with some ivory-colored ribbons. The cake board is covered in a striped ivory/gold fabric.

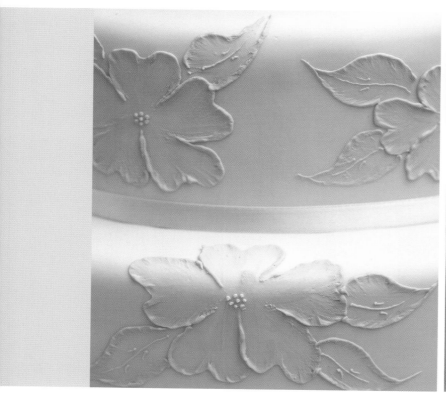

how-to techniques

BRUSH EMBROIDERY

Transfer the pattern to the cake using the same transfer technique as used on the Satin Stitch Monogram Cake (see page 64). Once the design is transferred, load a medium-size paper cone with a #2 or #3 round tip and Meringue Powder Royal Icing.

Start from the outside of the pattern and work your way toward the center of the pattern.

Outline a leaf by slightly dragging the tip to the surface. Before the outline dries, dip a #1 or #3 sable paintbrush in a little pasteurized egg white and carefully brush some of the outline icing toward the base of the leaf. Use long strokes to lightly brush a thin

layer of icing over the entire leaf pattern. The background should be visible through the layer. Continue to dip the brush in egg white and brush the outline icing, leaving the bulk of the outline icing intact. Continue with the rest of the leaves, brushing one leaf at a time. Let the leaves dry before beginning the petals. Remember to pipe one leaf at a time and one

From left to right: Beginning brush work on a transferred design on a sugar plaque; a finished brush embroidery flower.

petal at a time. Otherwise, the petals and leaves will dry before being
brushed with egg whites.

Outline one petal to start.
Before the outline icing dries, dip
the #1 or #3 sable paintbrush in
the egg white and lightly brush the
outline icing toward the center
of the flower. Use long strokes to
lightly brush a thin layer of icing
over the entire petal. Remember,
the background should be visible
through the icing. Brush the remaining petals, one at a time, until
all the petals are done. Take care
to maintain the integrity of each
petal—that is, its outline.

For the veining, load a #0 round
tip and Meringue Powder Royal
Icing in a small paper cone. Drag
the tip slightly from the base of
a leaf toward its point in a slight
curve. Go back to the slightly
curved line and pull out little veins
by inserting the tip and applying a
slight burst of pressure. Drag the
tip about ¼ in. (6 mm) and ease
off the pressure. Do this to the left
and right sides of the curved line.

Repeat this process for all the
leaves. For the center of the flower, position the #0 tip at the center
and pipe dots of icing in a rounded
cluster, forming stamens.

FOLIAGE

Making this foliage requires the
same technique as the leaf blades
in Chapter 2 (see page 32). The
difference is that the leaf blades
are cut freehand and the foliage in
this chapter uses a metal cutter.

From left to right: Wiring a base, cutting out a leaf, and a finished leaf blade.

cake 3

THE GROOM'S CAKE

This is a two-tier round cake covered in chocolate rolled fondant. The cake resembles a tuxedo. On the top tier, a section of the cake is covered in a tuxedo shirt, with buttons and a bow tie. The fondant shirt is ivory in color, and the shirt is textured with a satin rolling pin.

On the bottom tier, a section of the cake is covered with a vest. The fondant vest is a mocha color and is textured with a satin rolling pin. There is a gold button that keeps the vest closed, and a boutonniere is made up of a diamond design with a pressed rose on top.

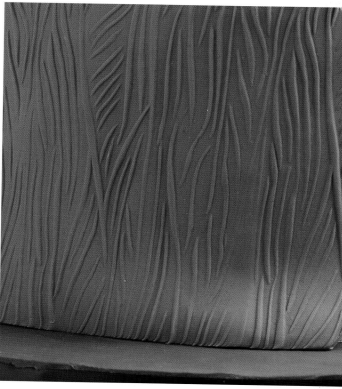

how-to techniques

TUXEDO SHIRT AND VEST

Rub a tiny amount of white vegetable shortening on a work surface and use a nonstick rolling pin to roll out 3 oz (85 g) of ivory-colored paste for the shirt and 4 oz (114 g) of brown-colored paste for the vest. Roll a textured rolling pin over the paste using the technique on page 23 to give a silk look to the shirt and vest. Cut out patterns for the tuxedo shirt and vest (see pages 250 to 251) and place over the textured paste. Carefully cut out the shirt and vest.

Place plastic wrap over the cut-out paste to prevent drying. Cover the remaining paste, which will be used for buttons later.

Turn both cut-out pieces of paste over and apply water or pasteurized egg white lightly with a pastry brush. Carefully attach

From bottom to top: Rolling out the gumpaste, texturing with a rolling pin, and cutting out a design resembling a tuxedo vest.

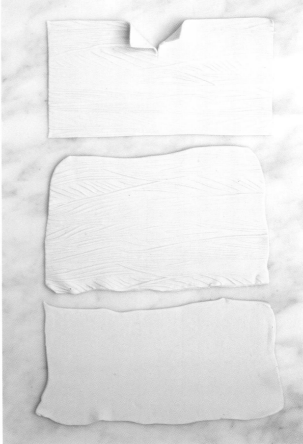

From bottom to top: Rolling out the ivory gumpaste, texturing with a rolling pin, and cutting out a design resembling a tuxedo shirt.

the shirt to the top tier, making sure it is centered and in front. Slightly turn the shirt collar down at a 45° angle. Attach the vest to the bottom tier, making sure it is centered and in front and in alignment with the shirt.

BUTTONS

Cut out buttons for the shirt using a #12 round metal tip. Attach to the shirt with Meringue Powder Royal Icing. Cut out a larger button for the vest with the opposite end of the #12

round tip. Attach with royal icing. Then take a small ball of paste and slightly flatten it. Paint with gold powder, mixed with a few drops of lemon extract. Once dried, attach the gold ball in the center of the vest's button with royal icing.

Using a metal round tip to cut out shapes for the shirt buttons.

From top to bottom: Finishing the vest button.

BOW

Trace the bow pattern (see page 252) along with the center strip and the detail strip. Rub a tiny amount of white vegetable shortening on a work surface and use a nonstick rolling pin to roll out 1 oz (28 g) of brown paste about $\frac{1}{16}$ to $\frac{1}{8}$ in. (1.5 to 3 mm) thick until thin. Dust a clean area of the work surface with a light coating of cornstarch and place all of the patterns over the brown gumpaste. Cut out the pieces and place plastic wrap over the pieces to prevent drying.

For the bow, brush a little water or pasteurized egg white in the center of the bow paste. Raise one end and attach it to the center of the bow strip. Attach the second end to the center of the bow strip. The bow is taking shape. Now brush a line of moisture in the center of the center strip. Attach the detail strip to that center. Then turn the center strip over and lightly moisten the back of the strip with water or pasteurized egg white. Place the center of the bow over the strip. Lap the ends over the center of the bow. Turn the bow over and tuck in the center with your thumb and middle finger. This helps shape and complete the bow. Let the bow dry for several hours, then attach the bow with royal icing to the bottom of the shirt.

From top to bottom: Cutting out a bow shape, overlapping the first side over, cutting out the center strip, and folding the center strip over to complete the bow.

BOUTONNIERE

Cut out a diamond shape of beige gumpaste. Let this dry. The boutonniere will be attached to this diamond.

Knead a small amount of brown gumpaste with a tiny amount of solid vegetable shortening. Press the paste into the rose press mold and release immediately. Let dry for 10 minutes. Carefully trim the excess paste from the pressed rose. Attach the pressed rose with a little Meringue Powder Royal Icing to the diamond shape. Let dry for 10 more minutes. Finally, attach the diamond to the vest with a little royal icing.

As another option, you could add the pressed rose without the diamond shield. Or you could use another shape as a background for the pressed rose, such as a daisy or scalloped shape, or an oval or round shape. The pressed rose can be entirely gilded or gilded on the edges.

Clockwise from top left: A rose press, texturing gumpaste in a press, cutting a diamond for the boutonniere, and the finished boutonniere.

CHAPTER FIVE

modern designs

Bold designs and pink and gray color combinations enhance these two extraordinary modern wedding cake designs. Inspired by a couple's active lifestyle, the cake artist can use geometric shapes, inventive patterns, and other highly visual design elements to truly represent a couple's personality in a contemporary cake design.

the couple

Tim and Brenda are a young, energetic couple who live in the Portland, Oregon area. Tim is a road construction engineer. He manages a staff of many that can be seen pouring asphalt and concrete and setting up warning signs for drivers. He is dedicated to his profession. For leisure, he is a member of a cycling group. Brenda works from home as a consultant for a software firm. She enjoys the flexibility because she is also an amateur marathon runner. She can be seen running for hours through the local streets and occasionally running though and around warning signs. This couple enjoys sitting by a log fire, sipping mulled cider, and talking about their day's events.

the consultation

The cake artist presents a portfolio and books on wedding cakes as well as a couple of sample tasting cakes and icings. The couple also brought in some pictures of cakes of their own. As the couple browses through the books and samples cake and icing, the cake artist takes out a notebook and jots down different designs of cakes that may interest the couple. The cake artist then takes out a sketch pad and begins to sketch rough designs based on the couple's interests.

elements of the cake

The couple can't decide between the Almond Paste Cake and the Dominican Cake. Both cakes are rich and delicious. The cake artist suggests the Almond Paste Cake for the top and bottom tiers and the Dominican Cake for the second tier. They have decided on a Pineapple Curd filling and the Italian Meringue Buttercream icing as a delicious undercoat icing for the rolled fondant. The first cake is three tiers. They are 6, 8, and 10 in. (15.2, 20.3, and 25.4 cm) and will serve 90 to 100 guests. The tiers are 4 in. (10.2 cm) high. The second cake is two tiers. They are 6 and 10 in. (15.2 and 25.4 cm) and will serve 50 to 60 guests. These tiers are 3 in. (7.6 cm) high.

development of the cake designs

The cake artist uses the sketches to come up with creative designs for the couple. The cake artist is aware that the couple might also wish to have a sheet cake for additional serving, in case they decide on the smaller wedding cake. The following two cake designs represent the cake artist's creativity during the development process:

CAKE 1: *The Triangular Cake*
The cake artist begins to sketch a
three-tier cake decorated with roads
and triangles. The cake artist is trying to tie in Tim's job and Brenda's
running. As this is a more modern/
retro design, the cake artist thinks of
designs that are more three-dimensional. Some triangles are drawn on
the sides of the cake, some on the
tiers, and the shoulder of the cake.
Some are triangles within triangles.
The color palette is pink and a bluish gray, which are the colors of the
wedding.

CAKE 2: *The Marbled Cake* The
cake artist plays on the same theme as
in Cake 1. This cake is smaller as the
couple is thinking of some economiz-
ing. This time the cake artist consid-
ers a marbleized design for the cake,
using the same color palette as in
Cake 1. The cake artist is thinking
along the lines of creating a top spray
of triangles and anthurium lilies.

cake 1

THE TRIANGULAR CAKE

This is a three-tier round cake enrobed in a pinkish rolled fondant. All three tiers are connected with intersecting roads. The roads are made from gumpaste and are gray with pink edging. There is a stitched line in the middle of the roads. The roads intersect in various directions, and some of the connections are covered with a triangle. The triangles are of different sizes and overlap in pink and gray. The triangles are angled in various directions, which gives edginess to the cake.

On top is a three-dimensional triangle with a gilded monogram. A pink ribbon extends from one of the triangles, which gives a soft look to counteract some of the sharpness of the cake.

how-to techniques

TRIANGLES

Rub a tiny amount of white vege-table shortening on a work surface and use a nonstick rolling pin to roll out 2 oz (57 g) of pink and gray gumpaste to $1/16$ in. (1.5 mm). Dust a clean area of the work surface with a light coating of cornstarch, put the paste on it, and cut out triangles in various sizes; let dry. When dried, attach some triangles on top of others in varying sizes with a little Egg White Royal Icing. Then attach the triangles to the cake in various directions.

Cutting and layering triangle shapes in contrasting colors.

DIFFERENT FLAVORS IN A TIERED WEDDING CAKE

A wedding cake can be made up of different layers and different flavors. A couple can have one or two tiers in a specific flavor and another tier in a different flavor. Or a couple can have different-flavored cake layers that make up a single tier. This can be complicated when trying to create just the right filling and icing to accommodate different layers.

If the couple has different flavors and cake for some tiers and different flavors and cake for other tiers, all of the guests won't get the chance to taste all of the layers and flavors. You can have extra sheet cakes in the kitchen and have them cut up and served with the wedding cake to give the guests a chance to sample all the different flavors of the wedding cake. However, this can be more expensive than having just one flavor and one cake.

ROADS

Cut out strips of gray gumpaste about 5 to 7 in. (12.7 to 17.8 cm) long and about 1 in. (2.5 cm) wide. Score a line down the middle of the strips with a quilting wheel. Cut strips of gumpaste in a pinkish color the same length as the roads and about ⅛ in. (3 mm) wide. Attach the strips to each side of the roads with a little pasteurized egg white. Then begin to assemble the roads on the cake in varying directions.

MONOGRAM

Trace the monogram and transfer it onto one of the triangles. Pipe the monogram with a #2 round tip and Meringue Powder Royal Icing in a small paper cone. Let dry for several hours. When dried, gild the monogram.

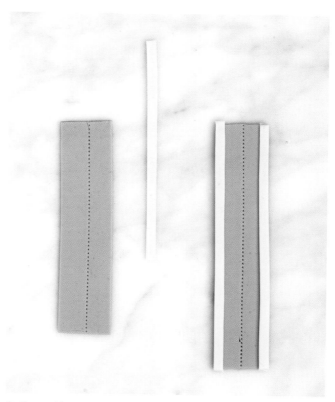

Cutting and layering strips of gumpaste in contrasting colors to make up roads.

cake 2

THE MARBLED CAKE

This is a two-tier cake that is marbleized with pink and gray rolled fondant. The color scheme is the same as that of the previous wedding cake, except the marbleizing gives the illusion of roads. This is a softer-looking cake without all the sharpness of the first cake design.

The top tier is decorated with a spray of white anthurium lilies and leaf blades. There is also a triangle spray on the cake board and on the top edge of the top tier.

how-to techniques

MARBLEIZING

Dust a work surface with a light coating of cornstarch and roll out a large circle of fondant in a pinkish color. Then add walnut-sized balls of gray fondant on top of the circle of pinkish fondant in random positions. Lightly roll with a large rolling pin, marbleizing the gray fondant into the pink fondant. Then add walnut-sized balls of pinkish fondant onto the gray sections of the rolled paste and continue to roll the paste to further marbleize the pink into the gray. Carefully pick up the paste onto a rolling pin and cover the cake with the marbleized paste.

ANTHURIUM LILY

For the spathe (petal), measure out 2 oz (57 g) gumpaste. You can leave it white or color it a bright or deep red, burgundy, pink, forest green, or bright yellow. Wrap the paste in plastic wrap to prevent drying. Also measure out 1 oz (28 g) of lemon-yellow paste for the spadix (base). Wrap in plastic wrap until ready to use.

For the spadix (base), form some of the yellow paste into an elongated cone. Dip a 24-gauge wire in egg white and insert it at the

From top to bottom: Adding round pieces of a contrasting color to rolled-out fondant, adding additional fondant in the original color, and rolling out the fondant to marbleize the colors.

wide end. Pinch to secure the paste to the wire. Allow to dry for several hours or overnight. When dried, brush the base in egg white and dip it in the cornmeal for pollen. Let dry for several more hours.

Rub a tiny amount of white vegetable shortening on a work surface and use a nonstick rolling pin to roll out the paste you set aside for the spathe until petal thin. Dust a clean area of the work surface with a light coating of cornstarch, transfer the paste to it, and carefully cut out the paste with a cutter or pattern (if using a pattern, the paste should remain on vegetable shortening). Cut out two more petals and cover them with plastic wrap to prevent drying.

Add texture and detail to the petals by placing them inside a silicone leaf press. For a waxy look, brush the front of the petals with egg white and let dry for 1 hour.

To assemble, place a petal brushed with egg white near the edge of a piece of Styrofoam. Using the wire from the cone, pierce the bottom of the petal about ½ in. (1.3 cm) from the base of the flower. Push the wire through the bottom of the petal until the base of the cone makes contact. The wire should extend through the Styrofoam and out the side for easy removal. Let dry for 24 hours.

Top, left to right: Making the spadix and coating in cornmeal. Bottom, left to right: Cutting and texturing the petal for an anthurium lily.

From top to bottom: Attaching the wired base to the petal to complete the anthurium lily.

wedgwood-inspired designs

Grand, sumptuous, blue/violet tones, lavish pipework, and country-inspired themes characterize these Wedgwood-inspired wedding cake designs. These cakes range from grand Jasperware-inspired designs in a Victorian style to a summer cottage theme, but each draws on the elegant characteristics of Wedgwood china.

the couple

Laura and Phil are a Canadian couple. They have been married for 10 years, and they wish to renew their vows. This is a unique couple that blends in everywhere they go. They are extremely wealthy, but they don't wear or show their wealth. Laura is a stay-at-home wife with lots of interests. She is an avid baker, she trains and breeds rare horses, and she manages their stately home and a 650-acre ranch in the mountains. She is a collector of fine china, and Wedgwood is her favorite. Phil is the CEO of a multi-billion-dollar investment consulting firm. He enjoys horseback riding and dirt biking in his spare time. The couple is not sure if they will be having a large wedding or a small private one.

the consultation

The couple is inspired by Wedgwood design, and they have brought some Wedgwood pieces with them as well as a couple of photos of cakes that are similar to what they are looking for. As the couple consults with the cake artist and looks through some additional books on cake art, the cake artist takes out a notebook and jots down some design concepts—some taken directly from some of the Wedgwood pieces—before starting to do some rough sketches.

elements of the cake

The clients have decided on the Lemon Pound Cake with a frozen raspberry puree filling and White Chocolate Buttercream icing under the Rolled Fondant. The first cake sketch is an 8-in. (20.3 cm) dome, the middle tier is an 8-in. (20.3 cm) round, and the grand tier is a 10-in. (25.4) round that is 8 in. (20.3 cm) high. There is a small support drum under the grand tier, which is a 12-in. (30.5 cm) round that is 1 in. (2.5 cm) tall. This cake serves 225 to 240 guests. The second sketch is three theirs. They are 6-, 8-, and 10-in. (15.2, 20.3, and 25.4 cm) rounds and serve 90 to 100 guests. The third cake is two tiers. They are 6 in. and 10 in. (15.2 and 25.4 cm) and serve 55 to 60 guests.

development of the cake designs

The cake artist is challenged by trying to incorporate Wedgwood designs into all three cake designs and make each cake design distinctly different. The cake artist slightly reworks some of the sketches to come up with three creative designs:

CAKE 1: *Victorian-Styled Cake*

The first sketch is quite grand. The cake artist starts out with a dome shape for the top tier and then draws the second tier that supports the top tier. The artist draws a large bottom tier, known as the *grand tier*, which is made up of smaller tiers. In the middle of the grand tier are cameos around the tier; around the bottom is drapery work. The cake artist isn't sure what type of pipework will be done, but that will be decided later as the cake artist develops this grand wedding cake.

CAKE 2: *Country Cottage Cake*

In this sketch, the cake artist draws on the color scheme to create a country cottage design, using cutouts, appliqué, and eyelet work. The cake artist draws three round tiers and draws appliqués as well as cornelli lace on the top and bottom tier. The cake artist hasn't decided exactly what to do on the middle tier but is thinking along the lines of doing eyelet work, along with appliqué work.

CAKE 3: *Color-Wash Cake*

In this sketch, the cake artist is thinking more rustic, using shades of Wedgwood blue and white. The cake artist is considering painting the top tier with shades of blue and white or piping a loose design on the top tier. The bottom tier might have some cornelli lace or sotas (similar to cornelli lace, only the lines are thicker and the embroidery overlaps in twists and circles) or Swiss dots on it; however, the cake artist hasn't decided yet. The top ornament will be a painted sugar bell.

cake 1

VICTORIAN-STYLED CAKE

T his grand design is inspired by the neoclassical style of Jasperware combined with the style of the late Victorian era. The cake is enrobed in violet rolled fondant with blue overtones. The concept here is violet/blue background with white appliqué and lavish pipework. The top has two tiers. The dome shape on top has textured leaf relief around the top and a rope border under the leaves. Under the dome is an 8-in. (20.3 cm) round cake with drapery design, hand-shaped rosettes, and blossoms.

The bottom tier is two tiers in one. The top is sectioned into eight V and crescent shapes. Overpiped half-circles are piped into the crescent-shaped designs, while blossoms overflow in the V-shaped designs. Overpiped V and crescent shapes extend beyond the design in descending order. Under the V and crescent designs are coat-of-arms and cameo designs. Below, near the cake board, is textured drapery work, flanked by hand-shaped rosettes and leaf relief.

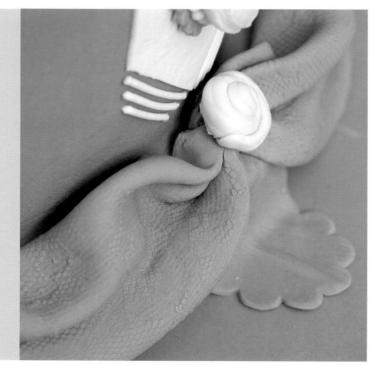
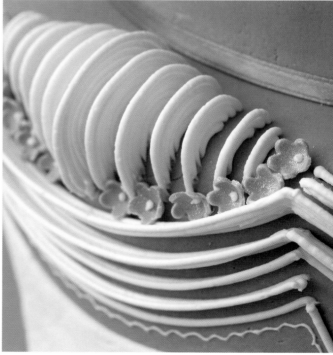

how-to techniques

CLASSIC DRAPERY

Rub a tiny amount of white vegetable shortening on your work surface. Using a nonstick rolling pin, roll out 4 oz (114 g) commercial rolled fondant or gumpaste on the shortening until thin.

Roll and trim the paste to a rectangle. Cut the rectangle into two or three strips, about 1½ × 6 in. (3.8 × 15.2 cm) and ⅛ in. (3 mm) thick. Turn the strips over to the fat side and brush the bottom of each with a little pasteurized egg white or water. Fold the dry side of each strip to the wet side,

developing a pillow or gathered effect.

Brush a little pasteurized egg white on one of the folded strips, just above the seam. Place another folded strip on the set seam. If using three strips, brush egg white on the seam of the second folded strip and attach the third strip.

Using a pastry brush, wet the area of the cake with a little water where the drapery is to appear. Pick up the folded strips by the ends. Shape the strips to the set surface on the cake. Break off any extended pieces with your fingers and secure the ends of the folded strips to the cake.

ROSETTES

Measure out 1 oz (28 g) of white gumpaste. Knead in a little white vegetable shortening into the paste. Roll the paste into a log and insert the log into a clay gun with the three-petal disk. Insert the plunger into the clay gun and apply a lot of pressure. A long rope will be expelled from the gun.

Cut the rope into 3-in. (7.6 cm) pieces. Take one of the pieces and tuck it into a tight circle. Repeat this for additional rosettes.

From top to bottom: Cutting a strip of gumpaste, folding over, and attaching one folded strip to another to form classical drapery.

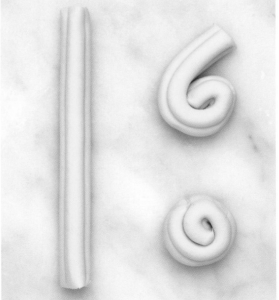

Clockwise from left: A rope of gumpaste from a clay gun, tucking and rolling the paste, a finished rosette.

TEXTURED LEAVES

Dust a work surface with a light coating of cornstarch and roll out 3 oz (85 g) of commercial rolled fondant or gumpaste until very thin. Cut out leaves with a cutter. Place the cutouts into a leaf press for texture. Apply a little pasteurized egg white on the backs of the leaves and attach the leaves around the bottom of the dome.

SHIELDS AND DIAMOND DISKS

Trace the pattern of the shield (see page 254). Roll out gumpaste about ⅛ in. (3 mm) thick on a work surface dusted lightly with cornstarch. Then place a piece of lace over the gumpaste. Roll over the lace firmly. Remove the lace. Place the pattern over the textured gum-paste and carefully cut out shields. Also cut out diamond disks with a diamond-shaped cutter. Apply the shields and diamond disks with pasteurized egg whites.

Textured leaves and drapery attached on the top two tiers.

Rolling lace over a cut-out shape to create a textured shield.

CAMEOS WITH OVAL DISKS

Knead about 2 oz (57 g) of gumpaste with a tiny amount of white vegetable shortening. Tear off about ½ oz (14 g) and shape it into an oval shape. Press the oval-shaped paste into the cameo mold. Turn the mold over and press firmly with the palm of your hand. Release the mold from the paste and let dry for 30 minutes. Carefully trim the cameo with an X-acto knife and brush the cameo with pearl luster.

Rub a tiny amount of white vegetable shortening on a work surface and use a nonstick rolling pin to roll out some blue gumpaste very thin. Cut out disks with a small oval cutter, just larger than the cameo. Allow to dry for 2 hours. When dried, attach the cameo to the oval-shaped disk with some royal icing. Pipe small beads around the cameo base with a #2 round tip. Then attach the cameo and disk to the shield with royal icing.

V- AND CRESCENT-SHAPED OVERPIPING

Begin by carefully measuring your cake. Use adding-machine paper to measure around the cake's circumference and divide the paper into sections or trace the V- and crescent-shaped patterns in the book as templates (see page 254). Measure from the top of the cake to the peak of the design. Use a pencil mark or pinprick at these key points so you will have a guide when piping.

Tilt your cake up by placing a small piece of Styrofoam or a small object under the cake (at 6 o'clock on the clock face). If you have a tilting turntable, tilt the cake to almost a 45° angle. Fill a pastry bag with Egg White Royal Icing and start with a #4 or #5 round metal piping tip. Pipe V and crescent shapes all around the cake. Since you are building up several lines of piping, you can pipe another line directly on top of the previous line. Continue until you have gone completely around the cake. Let this dry for 1 to 2 hours. The more you allow this to dry, the easier it will be to add more lines. Also, if you make a mistake, it's easier to remove the mistake when the

Pressing a gumpaste cameo in a cameo mold.

previous lines are already dry.

Pipe two to three lines with a #4 or #5 piping tip. Then change to a #3 round metal piping tip. Pipe two to three more lines, letting the lines dry for 1 hour between lines. Then change to a #2 round metal piping tip and pipe two lines.

Now pipe lines directly below the V and crescent shapes. The distance is 1/8 to 1/4 in. (3 to 6 mm). Repeat the technique of built-up lines. However, you want to decrease the number of lines as you build down.

For example, the first V and crescent shapes can have 6 to 8 lines. The line below will have two fewer lines, and the line below that two fewer lines, until you reach the last line, which has only a single line piped with a #2 piping tip.

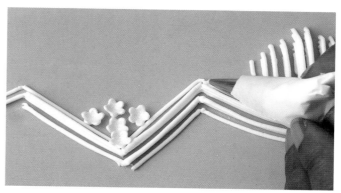

Building up the lines for V- and crescent-shaped overpiping.

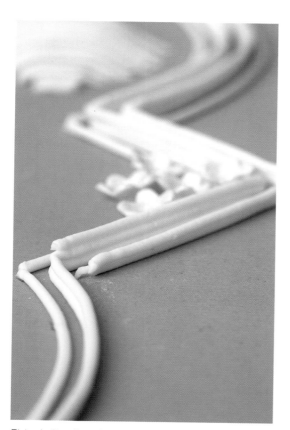

Piping built-up lines directly over each other for V- and crescent-shaped overpiping.

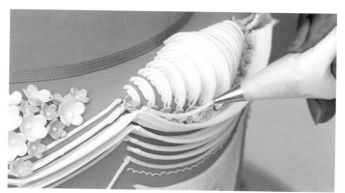

Piping the last built-up lines.

HALF-CIRCLE SHAPES

These go inside the crescent shape. It might be wise to do the half-circle shapes first and then do the V- and crescent-shaped overpiping.

First pipe three small curves with a #3 or #4 round metal tip, adding two more lines to the center curve. Let dry for 30 minutes. Pipe another line over all three curves. Let dry for 1 hour. Now pipe one line to the left and right of the three curves. Pipe an additional line on the three curves. Let dry for 1 hour. Change to a #2 piping tip. Pipe a line on all the curves. Let dry for 1 hour. Then pipe a new curve to the left and right of the five curved lines with a #2 piping tip. Pipe lines on the five curved lines. Let dry.

Continue with this pattern until you have filled up the crescent shape. You can pipe as many lines as you like to create depth.

PLUNGER FLOWERS

These are the blossoms that will fill up the cavity of the V shape.

Rub a tiny amount of vegetable shortening onto the work surface and roll out gumpaste with a nonstick rolling pin until it is petal thin. Transfer the paste to a surface dusted lightly with cornstarch.

Press the plunger cutter into the paste and move it back and forth to separate the petals from the rest of the paste. When you lift the cutter, the petals will be

attached to it. Place the cutter on a cell pad and press the plunger to release the cupped petals. Repeat this process until you have made as many flowers as you can.

Position the small ball of the dogbone tool at the edge of one of the petals. Gently pull the ball tool toward the center of the flower.

This thins the edge of the petal and further cups the flower. Go to the next petal and repeat the technique. Continue until the entire flower is complete.

To finish the flower, pipe a small dot of royal icing in the center with a PME #0 metal tip.

Attach flowers inside the V shape with dots of royal icing.

Building up half-circle lines.

Shaping a petal on a cell pad using a dogbone tool to create plunger flowers.

FREEHAND TEXTURED DRAPERY

Knead 8 oz (227 g) of commercial rolled fondant or gumpaste until it is pliable. Sprinkle the work surface lightly with cornstarch and roll out the paste into a loose rectangle, about 6 × 9 in. (15.2 × 22.9 cm) and ¹⁄₁₆ to ⅛ in. (1.5 to 3 mm) thick. Place a piece of lace over the paste and roll a rolling pin over the lace (as you did with the shield and diamond shapes). Remove the lace and square off the paste.

With a pastry brush and a little water, brush the area of the cake where the drapery will be placed. Fold under the top and bottom edges of the paste, about ½ in. (1.3 cm) in, to form a finished edge of your drape.

Pick up one end of the drape and gently gather it into soft folds. Then pick up the other end of the drape and do the same. Gently pick up the paste and gently pull it until it forms drapes. Carefully attach the drape to the damp area on the cake. Taper the ends of the paste and tear off any excess.

COMMERCIAL ROLLED FONDANT

Commercial rolled fondant has a small amount of vegetable gum already added to the paste to give the paste more flexibility and strength than rolled fondant made from scratch. Gumpaste is essentially commercial rolled fondant with additional vegetable gum added to give the paste even more flexibility and strength.

From left to right: Texturing a piece of gumpaste with lace.

Gathering the textured gumpaste and pulling on each end to form freehand drapery.

cake 2

COUNTRY COTTAGE CAKE

This cake is designed with appliqué and eyelet techniques. All three tiers are enrobed in a bluish rolled fondant. The top and bottom tiers are decorated with appliqué designs in wildflowers, azaleas, blossoms, and foliage. Some flowers are cutouts within cutouts, and some have negative spacing, which is filled with cornelli lace piping.

The middle tier is completely covered with white fondant (over the blue fondant), and tiny cutters are used to cut out shapes, revealing the blue fondant through the white cutouts. Some appliqué work is also applied here, and a scallop-shaped design is used on the top of the white fondant, giving it a shutter effect.

how-to techniques

APPLIQUÉ

Top and Bottom Tiers—The top and bottom tiers have cutouts of varying sizes and shapes. Roll out commercial rolled fondant on a work surface dusted lightly with cornstarch. Use several five-petal cutters, such as blossom and azalea type, in small and large sizes. Cut out the shapes and place plastic wrap over the shapes to prevent drying. Emboss the centers of some of the shapes with smaller blossom cutters and cut out the centers of some of the shapes.

Arrange the shapes and attach in a free style to the cake with a small amount of water on the back of each shape. Some shapes should curve to the shoulder of the cake, which gives an extension of the design.

Pipe cornelli lace in some of the shapes where the centers were cut out. Pipe freehand leaf shapes that extend the shapes of some of the flowers.

Center Tier—For the center tier, make a template by measuring the circumference and the height of this tier with parchment paper or heavy-duty construction paper. The template should be about ½ in. (1.3 cm) taller than the actual cake.

Use a nonstick rolling pin to roll out 2 lb (907 g) commercial rolled fondant or gumpaste on a work surface that has been rubbed with a tiny amount of white vegetable shortening. Roll out the paste into a large rectangular shape to ⅛ to ¼ in. (3 to 6 mm) thick. Place the template onto the paste and cut out carefully and quickly.

Cutting out appliqué flowers.

Cut out eyelet embroidery by using small blossom cutters and small round metal cutters to decorate the strip. Carefully turn the strip over and lightly dampen with water. Reverse the strip and carefully apply it to the middle tier.

Where the ends come together, pipe a little royal icing on the seam and use your fingertips to blend the icing to minimize the seam. Add appliqué pieces and embossing on the strip to further decorate the strip.

SHUTTERS

Rub a tiny amount of vegetable shortening on the work surface and use a nonstick rolling pin to roll out 3 oz (85 g) of white gumpaste to ⅛ in. (3 mm) thick. Trace the shutter pattern and place the pattern on the gumpaste. Carefully cut out with an X-acto knife and place pieces under plastic wrap until ready to use. Or use a round scallop cookie cutter as an alternative.

Drape the shutter pieces over the top edge of the strip. About ½ in. (1.3 cm) should be folded over the strip and secured with a little water. The next shutter piece should go right next to the previous one and so forth.

Using a small cutter to make eyelet embroidery.

cake 3

COLOR-WASH CAKE

This is a two-tier cake with a refreshing color-wash design. Both tiers are enrobed in white rolled fondant. The top tier is color-washed with gel food colors mixed with liquid whiteners to bring out the pastel tone of the colors. A paintbrush is dipped in the colors and then applied to the cake in a stucco fashion. This gives an antique Wedgwood look to the cake. Appliqué flowers are used around the shoulders of the top tier to pull together all of the colors in the wash. Fabric ribbon is used near the bottom of the cake to create a stylized look. On the top tier is a painted sugar bell decorated with fabric ribbons and blossoms.

The bottom tier is piped in cornelli lace. Fabric ribbon is used near the bottom of the cake to match the top tier. This is a small, intimate cake that can be served at the bridal party or just for the couple when they return from their honeymoon.

CHAPTER SEVEN

chocolate designs

Chocolate and pink are popular colors in clothing design, but they also appeal to couples whose passion for chocolate goes beyond the norm. Transparent drapery, beautiful fabric roses, and mouth-watering mini cakes are all a dream come true for chocolate lovers.

cake 1

CHOCOLATE AND PINK CAKE

This two-tier caked is enrobed in chocolate rolled fondant. The top tier is completely decorated with chocolate miniature roses made from a rose press. The top tier and cake board are also decorated with a cluster of pink star flowers with chocolate centers. The bottom tier has an almost transparent pink sugar drape that starts at the cake board and leads up to the bottom of the top tier. Sugar fabric roses are made to emulate the "quick" roses made from the rose press on the top tier, and pink and chocolate foliage accents the roses. The cake also has fine piping in pink that pulls the entire design together.

how-to techniques

PRESSED ROSES

This technique is exactly the same as that used for the boutonniere on the Groom's Cake in Chapter 4 (see page 77). It will take 65 to 75 pressed roses to fill the top tier of this wedding cake. It would be advisable to do about 20 at a time. Trim the roses after they have been released from the mold and then attach the pressed roses with a little water. Press them extremely close to each other.

Once this is complete, you might still have some "negative" spacing between some of the roses. Take some of the chocolate rolled fondant and make large pea-sized balls and press them individually into the center of the rose press. This will produce a miniature pressed rose. Use these to fill in the spaces.

FABRIC ROSES

Rub a tiny amount of white vegetable shortening on the work surface; then use a nonstick rolling pin to roll out 2 oz (57 g) pink commercial rolled fondant to about ⅛ in. (3 mm) thick on the work surface. Roll out the paste to a rectangle as if you are doing freehand drapery, which is discussed in the Victorian-Styled Wedding Cake in Chapter 6 (see page 101).

Square off the paste and cut a 6 × 4-in. (15.2 × 10.2 cm) strip. Fold under the top and bottom edges of the paste, about ½ in. (1.3 cm) in, to form a finished edge for your drape. Pick up the drape and slightly pull it. Then, using your left hand, turn the paste clockwise, forming a tight knot. Continue to turn with your left hand as you continue the tuck with your right hand in a counterclockwise motion. Seal the paste under the rose to hide the ends.

Holding both ends of a drape and turning it in a clockwise direction to make fabric roses.

TWO-TONE LEAVES

Rub a tiny amount of white vegetable shortening on a work surface and then use a nonstick rolling pin to roll out chocolate and pink commercial rolled fondant. Transfer to a clean area of the work surface dusted lightly with cornstarch and cut freehand or use a leaf cutter to make leaves. The chocolate leaves should be larger than the pink leaves.

Place a chocolate leaf in the bottom of the leaf press and then place a pink leaf directly on top of the chocolate leaf. Press the top of the leaf press, which creates the veining and glues the two leaves together.

Finish off the leaves with a little pinkish petal dust on top of the leaf.

Cutting, layering, and texturing leaves in dark chocolate and pink fondant to form two-toned leaves.

FREEHAND DRAPERY

Knead 8 oz (227 g) of commercial rolled fondant or gumpaste until it is pliable. Sprinkle the work surface lightly with cornstarch and roll out the paste into a loose rectangle, about 6×9 in. (15.2×22.9 cm) and $\frac{1}{8}$ to $\frac{1}{4}$ in. (3 to 6 mm) thick. Use two freehand drapes to drape the cake from the bottom of the bottom tier to the bottom of the top tier. Attach the first drape, then overlap the second drape over the previous drape to produce a more attractive look.

With a pastry brush and a little water, brush the area of the cake where the drapery will be placed. Fold under the top and bottom edges of the paste, about $\frac{1}{2}$ in. (1.3 cm) in, to form a finished edge of your drape.

Pick up one end of the drape and gently gather it into soft folds. Then pick up the other end of the drape and do the same. Gently pick up the paste and gently pull it until it forms drapes. Carefully attach the drape to the damp area on the cake. Taper the ends of the paste and tear off any excess.

cake 2

MINI-CAKES IN PINK AND CHOCOLATE

Arrangements of mini-cakes, 3 to 4 in. (7.6 to 10.2 cm) in diameter, are decorated in pink and chocolate. Some are iced in chocolate and some in pink. Fine pipework, ribbons, tulle, and hand-shaped flowers create an attractive arrangement of cakes, suitable for a wedding couple that wants individuality for each guest.

Piping Swiss dots onto a mini-cake.

how-to techniques

All of the techniques used for the mini-cakes have been discussed in previous chapters of the book.

Some of the mini-cakes are decorated with tiny blossoms and some freehand embroidery (see pages 100 and 51). Others have chocolate or pink ribbons that are ⅛ in. (3 mm) in diameter and are tied around the bottoms of the cakes for a finished look. Some have bows attached to the ribbons with dots of royal icing.

Some of the cakes have strips of commercial rolled fondant in pink or chocolate fitted around them, and some of the strips are textured with a textured rolling pin and then tied with ribbons (see page 23).

Some mini-cakes are decorated with Swiss dots, some with tulle with Swiss dots piped directly onto it, and some with gumpaste rosettes on top for a finished look (see pages 51 and 96).

seasonal designs

A unique palate of Tiffany blue, moss green, and white is the perfect combination for a Springtime theme, while bold, rustic colors like chocolate and orange and three-dimensional marzipan fruits create a harvest-inspired Fall feeling. For an earthy couple who love nature, the cake artist can draw inspiration from the seasons to create exciting cakes for any time of year.

the couple

Cindi and Tommy-Lee come from a rich cultural heritage. Their families are farmers who farm acres of corn, fresh vegetables, potatoes, and fruit; raise livestock; and produce fresh dairy products. This is a lifestyle of hard work, and both were born to this culture. At harvest, there is a bounty full of earthy goods, and in springtime, more bounty and fields of blossoms and flowers in a variety of vibrant colors perfume the air.

Cindi enjoys making homemade preserves and canning while she uses her bookkeeping skills to manage her family farm. Tommy-Lee is a skilled mechanic but enjoys making apple and peach wines from his family orchards. This couple is in love with nature and all that it provides to sustain life. They are thinking of a spring or fall wedding.

the consultation

This couple had a difficult time finding a skilled baker/decorator, other than cakes purchased from a local supermarket. They live in a rural area, and they had to travel to another state to find a cake artist. They had been looking through magazines trying to find a cake that would suit them, but they had a hard time finding that special cake. After looking through pictures and books and sampling cakes and icings, the couple couldn't decide on just one cake. So the cake artist made some notes on the styles and techniques that the couple loved and their background of farming to come up with some sketches.

elements of the cake

The couple enjoyed the Red Velvet Cake at the sampling during the consultation. The cake artist suggested pairing the Red Velvet Cake with white chocolate Ganache and Cream Cheese Buttercream under the Rolled Fondant. The first sketch is of a square cake with 6- and 10-in. (15.2 and 25.4 cm) tiers that will serve 70 to 80 guests. The second sketch is a round cake with 6- and 10-in. (15.2 and 25.4 cm) tiers and serves 55 to 60 guests.

development of the cake designs

The cake artist pulls the sketches drawn and dresses them up to create two unique styles of cake for this loving couple. The following two cakes represent the cake artist's creativity during the development process:

CAKE 1: *The Cake with Lily and Pleats* In this sketch the cake artist draws on the fact that the couple is looking for rich color combinations in greens, blues, oranges, and browns. The cake artist draws a two-tier square cake. Both tiers are decorated with appliqué flowers, and the color of the tiers is a mint green. The artist isn't sure where to use other colors at this time but is considering some type of blue to go with the mint green for a springtime look.

CAKE 2: *Rustic Cake with Marzipan Fruits* In this sketch the cake artist draws a two-tier round cake. The artist is thinking about a fall theme with oranges and browns. The artist draws maple leaves in two-toned color combinations to decorate the cake but isn't sure what type of ornament will adorn the top of the cake at this time.

cake 1

THE CAKE WITH LILY AND PLEATS

This is a two-tier square cake enrobed in mint-green rolled fondant. Both tiers are decorated with a gathered pleat at the bottom of the cake in Tiffany blue. The pleats signify a "picket fence" around a warm home. The top tier is tied with a transparent ribbon, while the bottom tier is tied with a mint-green ribbon.

Appliqué flowers decorate the sides of each tier and on the top tier are two white tiger lilies, hand shaped from gumpaste.

The tiers are set on a rectangular drum that matches the mint-green color of the cake.

how-to techniques

TIGER LILY

First, begin by making the six stamens and one pistil needed to complete the center of the flower. To make the stamens, roll a pea-sized amount of white gumpaste into a tiny ball. Brush a length of 28-gauge white florist wire with egg white and thread the ball to the center of the wire. Place the wire and ball on the work surface and roll the ball back and forth with your middle finger, stretching the paste against the wire. Continue to roll the paste, using more fingers as it stretches. When the paste extends beyond the reach of your fingers, place the paste and wire between your hands and rub them back and forth to stretch the paste along the length of the wire. Continue to roll the paste until it extends beyond the wire. The paste will be extremely thin against the wire. Break off any excess and slightly curve the wired paste for a natural form. This is the first stamen. Make six more.

To create the pistil, take one of the stamens and add a tiny piece of brown paste at the end of it. This stamen should be longer than the other stamens. Shape the pistil to a natural curve and let dry overnight. Once dry, petal-dust the stamens lightly with mint green and petal-dust the top of the pistil with chocolate-brown petal dust. Then surround the pistil with the other six stamens and tape them together with florist tape. Open the stamens for a more natural look.

For the petals, roll ¼ oz (7 g) gumpaste into a 3-in. (7.6 cm) log. Dip a 24-gauge wire in egg white and insert about ½ in. (1.3 cm) deep into one end of the log.

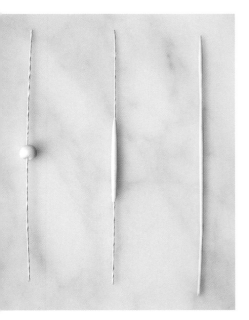

From left to right: Rolling gumpaste and placing on a wire, rolling out the gumpaste, and a finished stamen for a tiger lily.

From left to right: Rolling a ball of gumpaste into a log, wiring the log and rolling out to create a petal.

From left to right: Cutting and texturing a petal for a tiger lily.

Pinch to secure the paste to the wire. Place the wired log on a work surface rubbed with a tiny amount of vegetable shortening and flatten the center of the log with a nonstick rolling pin. Roll the paste on either side of the centered wire with a modeling stick. Follow the rest of the procedure as used for the leaf blade in Chapter 2 (see page 32) or use a tiger lily cutter to cut out the petals.

To texture the petals, press a corn husk or leaf former (also known as leaf press) onto the petal to create lines. Lightly soften the edge of the petal with a dogbone tool, but be careful not to ruffle it. Drape the petal over a nonstick rolling pin and allow it to dry. Make five more petals.

Lightly dust each petal with mint-green petal dust (near the bottom of the petal) and lightly brush the edge of the petal with the same color. Since these are white tiger lilies, only a hint of green is used. Then brush each petal with super pearl to give luster to each of the petals.

For the dots on the petals, dip a toothpick in mint-green food color and blot the color on a piece of paper towel. Carefully add dots to the petals, starting near the bottom of the petal and working your way up toward the center of the petal. Re-dip the toothpick and continue to add dots to the remaining five petals.

To assemble the flower, attach the first three petals to the center spray of stamens and tape securely. Add the last three petals at the seams and tape securely. Open the petals and stamens for a more natural look.

Taping two petals of a tiger lily together with florist tape.

A complete tiger lily, with 6 petals, 6 stamens, and 1 pistil taped together in the center of the flower.

GATHERED PLEATS

To start, rub a tiny amount of vegetable shortening on the work surface. Use a nonstick rolling pin to roll out 2 oz (57 g) gumpaste and cut it to about 2 × 8 in. (5.1 × 20.3 cm) and about ⅛ in. (3 mm) thick. Pick up the paste and place it on a clean area of the work surface dusted with a little cornstarch to prevent sticking.

To gather the "fabric," you will need a number of lollipop sticks or skewers. Place the first stick or skewer under the paste. Place the second stick on top of the paste, next to the first stick. Place the third stick underneath the paste, next to the second stick. The gathers are starting to form.

Continue placing lollipop sticks until all the paste is gathered. Let the paste set for 15 to 20 minutes. Remove the sticks to reveal the gathers.

Attach the gathers to the cake with a little water or pasteurized egg whites.

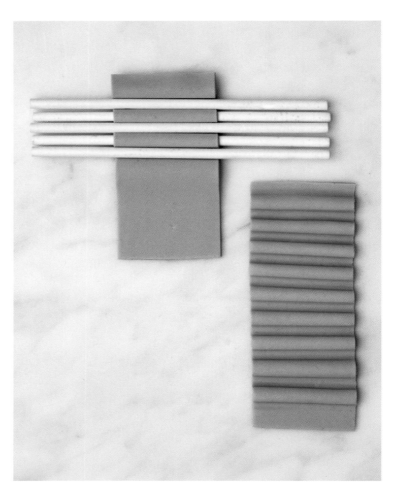

From left to right: Placing skewers above and below a piece of gumpaste and pressing tightly together to form gathered pleats; the finished pleats.

APPLIQUÉ FLOWERS

Rub a tiny amount of vegetable shortening on the work surface and use a nonstick rolling pin to roll out ½ oz (14 g) blue gumpaste petal thin. Place the gumpaste on a clean area of the work surface dusted with a little cornstarch and cut out petals with a four-petal metal cutter. Place aside.

Make up plunger flowers using the technique described in Chapter 6 (see page 100). Pipe a green center in each plunger flower with a PME #0 tip and mint-green royal icing.

Attach the petals to the cake with a little water; then attach the plunger flowers to the petals with a dot of royal icing.

From left to right: Cutting out a small white blossom and a blue star-shaped blossom, attaching the blossoms together to make appliqué flowers.

cake 2

RUSTIC CAKE WITH MARZIPAN FRUITS

This is a two-tier round cake. The bottom tier is enrobed in orange rolled fondant, and the top tier is covered in brown rolled fondant. Maple leaf foliage in marbleized brown and orange adorns both tiers and is attached with red berries.

The bottom tier is tied with brown tulle with a bunch of red berries in the bow, and the top tier overflows with almost-life-size marzipan lemons, peaches, pears, oranges, apples, and raspberries, all hand-shaped.

The cake is set on a round, orange fondant-covered drum with additional foliage around the base.

how-to techniques

TWO-TONE LEAVES AND BERRIES

For two-tone leaves, roll out ½ oz (14 g) brown marzipan. Then roll out a large pea-sized amount of orange marzipan into round balls and place the balls onto the brown marzipan. This is the same technique used in marbleizing, which is shown in Chapter 5 (see page 88).

Roll the rolling pin over the paste, combining the orange and brown paste together. Cut out with a maple leaf cutter.

Place the leaves under a leaf press for a more natural look.

For berries, roll tiny amounts of red paste into miniature balls and attach to the maple leaves with a drop of water.

MARZIPAN FRUITS

Orange Measure out 1 to 2 oz (28 to 57 g) of orange marzipan. Knead a pea-sized amount of green marzipan into the orange for depth and shadow. Place the paste in your nonwriting hand and put your writing hand directly on top. Rotate your hands in opposite directions until the paste forms a round ball.

Rounding off the marzipan to make an orange.

Adding texture to the orange using a cheese grater.

Indenting the top of the orange and placing a sliver of clove in the indentation to form the stem and complete the orange.

Roll the ball of paste over a cheese grater to give it an orange-like texture. Do not apply too much pressure, as you want to maintain the ball shape. Next, to soften the texture, lightly rotate the ball between your hands.

Place the paste on the work surface. With the small end of a dogbone tool, press lightly on the top of the ball to form a slight indentation. Place a small clove in the center of the indentation and push it until it is flush with the orange. This is the stem of the orange.

The orange is complete. However, you can add depth to its appearance by dusting the orange lightly with a sable paintbrush dipped in orange petal dust. For even more depth, blend a little moss-green petal dust near the stem of the orange.

Lemon Add a pea-sized amount of green marzipan paste to 1 to 2 oz (28 to 57 g) of lemon-yellow marzipan paste. Knead the colors together for a more natural tone.

Place the paste in your non-writing hand and place your writing hand directly on top. Rotate your hands in opposite directions until a ball forms.

Roll the ball of paste over a cheese grater for a textured surface as you did for the orange. Use your fingers to hold the textured ball in your nonwriting hand. With the thumb and index finger of your writing hand, pinch the top of the ball to a dull point and rotate the paste back and forth. Reverse the paste so the dull point is on the bottom. Pinch the paste again to form another dull point. The lemon is starting to take shape.

Hold the lemon at one end and score the other end with an X-acto knife, pressing the knife into the middle of the dull point, turning the paste one-quarter turn, and pressing the knife again, forming a cross. Press a tiny clove sliver in the center of the cross for the lemon's stem.

Hold the lemon at each end and gently push the paste toward the center. The lemon is complete.

For greater depth, lightly dust the lemon with lemon-yellow petal dust and a little moss-green petal dust near the stem.

Granny Smith Apple Knead together 1 oz (28 g) green marzipan to $\frac{1}{2}$ oz (14 g) of lemon-yellow marzipan. Roll the paste into a ball. Place the ball on the work surface and place your hands on either side of the ball of paste. Press your hands together. Apply pressure with the pinkie fingers to narrow the bottom of the paste. Continue to apply pressure to make the bottom of the paste smaller. Alternatively, pick up the paste with your nonwriting hand and pinch one end as you rotate the ball left and right. Next, turn the paste over so the round part is on top. The apple shape is developing but needs refinement. The paste should look like a hot-air balloon—wide on top but very narrow on the bottom.

Rolling out marzipan to make a Granny Smith apple.

Shaping the apple.

Applying pressure to both sides of the marzipan apple at the bottom to make an apple shape.

Making a cavity on top of the apple using a cone and serrated tool.

Softening the cavity of the apple with a dogbone tool for a more natural look.

Adding a sliver of clove for the stem of the apple.

Next, place the cone side of a cone and serrated tool directly in the center of the apple. Push the tool ¼ to ½ in. (6 mm to 1.3 cm) into the apple. This expands the center of the apple and condenses the overall shape of the ball. Next, soften the shoulder of the apple with a dogbone tool. To do this, position the tool inside the cavity of the apple and rotate the tool, starting with the smallest ball. When you reach the top of the apple, switch to the larger ball and continue to rotate until the shoulder of the apple is smooth. Place

a long curved clove sliver in the center of the apple.

For the leaf, roll out a walnut-sized piece of green marzipan on a little cornstarch as thinly as possible. Cut out a petal using a calyx cutter; then cut each sepal away from the center.

Pick up one tiny sepal and pinch the square end to shape a tiny leaf. Attach the leaf inside the cavity of the apple, opposite the stem, with a little water.

For a more dramatic look, brush a little pinkish petal dust on each cheek of the apple.

Cutting out marzipan with a calyx cutter to make a leaf for the marzipan apple.

Separating one of the sepals from the cut-out calyx to make a leaf for the marzipan apple.

Adding the leaf to the marzipan apple.

fashion-inspired designs

Fashion colors and attire from classic films provide the perfect source of inspiration for elegant, pristine wedding cake designs. Classic Australian stringwork makes a yellow and white daisy cake hard to resist, while the drapery and modern details on a sexy black and white cake call to mind an "open" dress with a twist. "Stunning" is the only word to describe these gems.

the couple

Barbara and Ken are a savvy couple from the San Francisco/Oakland area. They enjoy the sidewalk cafés, the colorful houses, and the different districts and attractions that San Francisco offers. On Sundays, they drive across the Bay Bridge to Oakland and stroll around Lake Merritt.

Barbara is a clothes merchandiser for a large department store in San Francisco. She has her finger on the pulse of fashion and colors. For relaxation she collects beads and turns them into fashion accessories, and she also enjoys fine needlework on pillow cushions.

Ken is an architect and works for a consulting firm. To unwind, he is a member of a sports club where he enjoys boxing and racquetball. At night he enjoys film noir and other classic films from the 1930s and 1940s.

The couple is looking for that special wedding cake to make their day memorable.

the consultation

The couple is inspired by modern fashion colors and film noir, and they have some ideas about color schemes, such as black and white or yellow and white. This is a small, intimate wedding, and the couple is really looking for something striking. They even brought in a picture of a dress they saw in an old movie as an inspiration. As the couple consults with the cake artist and looks through some additional books on cake art, the cake artist takes out a notebook and jots down some design concepts—some taken directly from popular magazines that show beautiful color combinations—before starting to do some rough sketches.

elements of the cake

The couple has decided on the Lemon Coconut Cake with Lemon Curd filling and Swiss Meringue Buttercream icing under the Rolled Fondant. The first sketch is of a two-tier round cake. The sizes of the tiers are 6 and 10 in. (15.2 and 25.4 cm), and the cake serves 55 to 60 guests. The second sketch is also rounded, and the tier sizes are the same as in the first sketch; this cake will also serve up to 60 guests.

development of the cake designs

The cake artist uses the sketches to come up with creative designs for the couple. The following two cakes represent the cake artist's creativity during the development process:

CAKE 1: *Yellow and White Cake* In this sketch the cake artist plays with the yellow and white concept. Both tiers are yellow with daisies decorating both tiers. On the top tier, the cake artist draws a spray of daisies and ribbons.

CAKE 2: *Black and White Cake* The cake artist sketches a two-tier cake. Around the bottom and top tiers are rows of piped beads. The cake artist is thinking simple, modern, but elegant. The top tier is black, and the bottom is white. This gives the effect of a black-and-white film. The sketch also shows a lavish drape around the shoulder of the top tier with a magnificent bow.

YELLOW AND WHITE CAKE

This elegant two-tier round cake is an example of fine piping with lots of details. The tiers are covered in lemon/egg-yellow rolled fondant. The bottom tier is piped and decorated in classic Australian stringwork, which gives the cake a lacy and delicate look. Freehand embroidery pipework is above the stringwork.

The top tier has an arrangement of daisies, mimosas, and foliage with ribbons. Appliqué daisies decorate the sides of both top and bottom tiers.

how-to techniques

AUSTRALIAN STRINGWORK

Marking the Cake To mark a cake, wrap a strip of adding machine paper around the circumference of the cake. Measure the paper carefully so the ends meet around the cake but do not overlap. Fold the strip in half four times to create 16 equal sections.

Use the following chart to determine the width of the paper strip. Cut off any excess width.

cake height	height of strip
3 in. (7.6 cm)	1 ¼ in. (3.2 cm)
4 in. (10.2 cm)	1 ½ in. (3.8 cm)
5 in. (12.7 cm)	1 ¾ in. (4.4 cm)

Position a rounded cookie cutter or a large glass at one end of the folded strip and draw a curve from one edge of the strip to the other. Carefully cut on the curved line. When the cut strip is unfolded, it will have a scalloped edge.

Attach the paper around the cake, about ¼ in. (6 mm) above the bottom, with the scalloped edge down and the straight edge up. Secure the paper to the cake with masking tape or stickpins.

Score the top edge of the paper with a quilting wheel; this is where the extension work will begin. Then score the scalloped bottom of the paper; this is where the bridgework will begin and the extension work ends. Remove the paper from the cake.

Piping 5 to 7 lines next to each other with a #3 round tip and Egg White Royal Icing, to make the bridge for Australian stringwork.

Brushing the bridge with Flood Icing to strengthen and smooth it.

Making the Bridge Using 1 oz (28 g) Egg White Royal Icing, pipe a snail's trail (also called a *bead* or *oval border*) around the bottom of the cake with a #5, #6, or #7 round metal tip, or use a thin ribbon to cover the bottom edge of the cake. For the bridgework, use a #3 round tip. Pipe the first row of the scalloped bridge following the mark made by the quilting wheel. Once you've gone completely around, pipe the next row above and parallel to the first. Build the scalloped lines outward five to seven times.

To smooth the bridge, brush 1 oz (28 g) of Flood Icing over it to cover any cracks and spaces between the piped lines. Let dry for 1 hour or overnight.

Extension Work Rebeat 1 oz (28 g) of Egg White Royal Icing by hand in a small ramekin or use a metal offset spatula to smash the icing against a flat surface to get rid of lumps. Cut a small paper cone, fit it with a PME #0 metal tip, and load the rebeaten icing.

Starting at the top of the scored line, position the tip and touch the cake. Apply a burst of pressure at the start, creating a dot; then squeeze and pull the tip upward.

Hold the string for a brief moment to dry slightly. Then bring the tip to the bottom of the bridge and break off the icing or move the tip slightly under the bridge to break off. It is important to predict the length of the string by measuring the distance from the top of the line to the bottom of the bridge.

The strings should be $1/16$ to $1/8$ in. (1.5 to 3 mm) apart. Continue until you have completed the stringwork.

EXTENSION WORK AND STRINGWORK

Extension work and *stringwork* are interchangeable terms. Both are used to describe this classic Australian technique. Note that the extension work is piped with Egg White Royal Icing. While you can do extension work with pasteurized egg white, it is not as strong, and often there are tiny air bubbles visible to the naked eyes on the strings.

Piping tiny strings through a #0 metal tip, to form stringwork.

DAISIES

Make the foundation of the daisy by rolling a large pea-sized amount of gumpaste in your hands. Then shape the foundation into a cone by applying a little pressure at one end of the ball.

Next, make a hole in the rounded part of the ball using a modeling stick. Then stretch the cavity by applying pressure with the modeling stick, rolling the stick back and forth on a work surface, forming a wide-brimmed hat.

Place the daisy cutter over the wide-brimmed hat and cut out the flower. This is the bottom of the daisy. Shape the flower by placing it on a cell pad and shape the back of each petal using a dogbone tool. Then turn the flower over and carefully vein the center of each petal with a veining tool or a toothpick.

Wire the flower by placing a 24-gauge wire that has been dipped in egg white through the front of the flower and into the cavity. Secure the bottom of the trumpet to the wire.

Place on Styrofoam to dry as you make the top of the daisy.

For the top petal, rub a tiny amount of white vegetable shortening on a work surface and use a nonstick rolling pin to roll out a small amount of gumpaste as thin as possible. Transfer the rolled-out paste to a clean area of the work surface dusted with a light coating of cornstarch. Cut several petals with the same cutter used to make the foundation. Cover the petals with plastic wrap to prevent drying.

Take one of the petals and shape

From top to bottom: Shaping a gumpaste cone and using a modeling stick to stretch the cone into a wide-brimmed hat.

Placing a cutter over the wide-brimmed hat to cut out the foundation of a daisy.

Wiring and assembling a daisy.

it with a dogbone tool and vein the center of each petal with a toothpick or a veining tool as done with the foundation petal.

Apply a little pasteurized egg white to the center of the foundation. Then apply one of the petals to the foundation, taking care to place the petal in the negative spacing between the foundation petals.

Then take a pea-sized amount of yellow gumpaste and form it into a round ball. Slightly flatten the tiny ball of paste and attach it to the center of the daisy with a little egg white. Brush the yellow

center with a little egg white and dip the yellow center into yellow cornmeal (to form pollen). The daisy is complete.

APPLIQUÉ DAISIES

These daisies use exactly the same procedure as the daisies just described, except there is no support base and no wires.

Cut two petals with a daisy cutter and shape and vein the flower as you did when making the daisies. Attach the petals together

and place a yellow center dipped in cornmeal to the center of the daisy. Attach to the cake with a dot of royal icing.

MIMOSAS

Roll out pea-sized amounts of yellow gumpaste. Insert a 28-gauge wire into egg white and ease the wire into the yellow paste. Let dry. When dried, brush the wired paste with egg white and dip into cornmeal to form pollen.

Cutting the top petal of a daisy, which will be shaped and fluted.

The complete daisy, with a yellow center that has been dipped in cornmeal to form pollen.

From left to right: Rolling a small yellow ball of gumpaste to make a mimosa, wiring the gumpaste, and dipping the ball in cornmeal to form pollen.

cake 2

BLACK AND WHITE CAKE

This is a sexy two-tier round cake that represents a cocktail dress. The top tier is enrobed in black rolled fondant and the bottom tier in white.

On the top tier is a dramatic gumpaste drape, which lies off the shoulders of the cake and is brought together with a gathered and pleated bow with a hand-pressed rose and ribbon streamers.

The bottom tier has a modern accent to it. Black and white buttons are attached at an angle on the cake. A triangle-cut gumpaste ornament is attached to the cake; it represents the dress "slightly opened." Inside the dress is hand-piped Australian stringwork with black "hailspotting" on the strings. Stringwork is also attached to the ornament.

how-to techniques

BOW

Creating the bow combines techniques already learned, such as making gathered pleats to form the texture of the bow and pulling both ends of the bow to the center to make the bow shape. Review the techniques for gathered pleats in Chapter 8 (see page 128).

Once the pleats are gathered and the skewers removed, the pleats should be at least 6 to 8 in. (15.2 to 20.3 cm) in length and about 3 in. (7.6 cm) wide. Pull both ends of the pleats to the center of the bow. Use a little pasteurized egg white to hold the ends together. Gently squeeze the center of the pleats to create a bow-tie look. Carefully turn the bow over so the ends of the bow are now underneath. Pinch the center again to form a more attractive bow.

Create a small rose using the rose press technique in Chapter 7 (see page 116) and place in the center of the bow. Petal-dust the rose with pearl luster for the completed bow.

From top to bottom: Gathering a piece of gumpaste, folding toward the center, and turning the bow over and tucking the gumpaste underneath to make a gathered bow.

DRAPERY

The drapery on this cake is the same technique used on the Chocolate and Pink Cake in Chapter 7 and on the Victorian-Styled Cake in Chapter 6 (see page 96).

BUTTONS

Roll out small amounts of black and white gumpaste. Cut out black buttons using the large end of a #199 tip, and cut out the white overlap buttons using the cut-edge end of the #199 tip. Attach both buttons with a little water and attach to the cake with a dot of royal icing.

STRINGWORK

Review the procedures for Australian stringwork on the Yellow and White Cake in this chapter (see page 144). Using 1 oz (28 g) Egg White Royal Icing, pipe a small crescent curve near the bottom of the cake, about 2 in. (5.1 cm) in length, with a #3 round tip. Overpipe the crescent curve to build up three lines. Pipe the extension strings with a PME #0 tip. Once done, fill a small paper cone with black royal icing that has been thinned down with a few drops of water. The icing should have a "flood" consistency, as discussed in Australian Stringwork (page 144).

Snip the end of the paper cone with black icing and begin to pipe the dots. To pipe the dots, slightly squeeze the bag and allow the icing to barely come out of the cone. Touch the icing to the string and immediately pull the bag toward you. Move down the line of the strings and pipe three dots evenly spaced. Then skip a line and pipe three more dots.

TRIANGLE SKIRT WITH STRINGWORK

Attach the triangle skirt at an angle that separates the buttons and the stringwork. Attach the triangle with royal icing and hold the triangle for 10 to 20 seconds so that it does not fall into the stringwork and break the pipework. Let dry for 1 hour.

Once dried, pipe stringwork from the cake directly onto the skirt. Be careful when attaching the ends of the stringwork to the skirt.

CHAPTER TEN

floral designs

*Creamy colors, hand-shaped white chocolate roses, pretty
stenciling, a monochromatic ribbon bouquet, and sumptuous
piping are the hallmarks of these delightful cakes. Inspired
by a couple's love of flowers, pottery, and antiques, the cake
artist is able to portray the couple's passion for details and love
of summery floral colors in an array of beautiful cakes.*

the couple

Henry and Martha live in the Boston/New England area. They were born and raised there. They are a middle-aged couple, and both have been married before. They are sea lovers, and they enjoy great seafood. Their eyes met at a local flower show, and they have been inseparable ever since.

Henry owns a successful automobile dealership. Before he leaves for work each day, he can be seen working in his garden, pruning and growing beautiful flowers. They are truly his pride and joy.

Martha is an art teacher at a local high school, and is planning to open up a pottery shop and teach pottery making. Recently she was handed down a family heirloom—an antique vase in brown, gold, green, and pink. The vase is decorated sumptuously and gilded. This has become her most prized possession.

Martha and Henry aren't completely sure what they want for their wedding cake, but they are looking for something special that reflects their love of flowers, pottery, and antiques.

the consultation

The cake artist presents a portfolio and books on wedding cakes, just to give the couple a starting point, as well as a few sample tasting cakes and icings. As the couple consults with the cake artist and looks through some additional books on cake art, the cake artist takes out a notebook and jots down some design concepts before starting to do some rough sketches.

elements of the cake

The couple has decided on the Peanut Butter Cake with a raspberry puree filling and a Praline Mocha Buttercream icing under the Rolled Fondant. The first cake is made up of 6-, 9-, and 12-in. (15.2, 22.9, and 30.5 cm) rounds and serves 125 to 132 servings. The second cake is made up of 6-, 8-, and 10-in. (15.2, 20.3, and 25.4 cm) rounds and serves 95 to 100 guests. The third cake is made up of 6-, 7-, 8-, and 9-in. (15.2, 17.8, 20.3, and 22.9 cm) rounds and serves 115 to 122 guests.

development of the cake designs

The cake artist uses the sketches to come up with creative designs for the couple. The following three cakes represent the cake artist's creativity during the development process:

CAKE 1: *Crown of Petals Cake*

The cake artist draws a three-tier cake and envisions this cake on a somewhat lavish scale. The top and bottom tiers are in a gold tone, and the middle tier is between a moss-green and mint-green color. The artist draws flowers around the top tier, envisioning a crown of petals, somewhat similar to what was on the vase. There are petals around the bottom of the second tier and some drop stringwork on the middle tier.

CAKE 2: *Peaches and Cream Cake* This sketch has a simpler look, with hand-shaped roses and foliage on top and a ribbon spray on the bottom of the second tier.

CAKE 3: *Cascade Ribbon Cake* This sketch has an even simpler look. The color scheme is monochromatic with Swiss dots on each tier. The artist is thinking of adding a sugar ribbon bouquet on the top tier.

CROWN OF PETALS CAKE

This is a three-tier round cake in a somewhat lavish piped floral style. The top and bottom tiers are covered in butterscotch/gold rolled fondant, and the middle tier in a moss/mint-green rolled fondant. The top tier has a crown of piped petals and leaves in pink, lavender, and mauve with clusters of moss-green dots. The middle tier has a crown of half-moon pastillage disks spaced about ½ to ¾ in. (1.3 to 1.9 cm) apart. The disks are a pinkish color. Stringwork is piped around the middle of the disks, and drop stringwork is piped below the pink disks, with connecting stringwork. The bottom of the second tier is covered with a ring of gumpaste blossoms and green foliage.

The bottom tier has overpiped work near the shoulder of the cake with cornelli lace piping, and the bottom of the cake is finished with a piped ribbon and decorated with cornelli lace and blossoms with green foliage.

There is a separate knife corsage decorated with purple/pink blossoms, buds and foliage, and ribbons in pink, mint green, and purple.

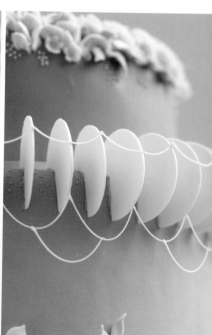

how-to techniques

CROWN OF PETALS

The top edge of the top tier requires several techniques to complete the floral crown.

First: Sweet Pea Clusters To begin, load a pastry bag with pinkish royal icing and a #102 petal-shaped tip. Position the tip at a 45° angle to the shoulder of the cake with the wide end touching. Apply a burst of pressure, allowing some icing to flow through the tip. Drag the tip to the surface as you pull the tip toward you. Angle the back of the tip up as you ease the pressure and stop. This is called a *flute*. Now position the tip at the upper left or right of the flute, the wide end of the tip touching the surface. Slightly angle the tip to a 45° angle. Apply a burst of pressure as you drag the tip to the tail end of the flute. Stop the pressure and pull the tip toward you. Now position the tip at the opposite side of the flute and repeat the squeeze-and-pull technique. You now have a small sweet pea cluster. Repeat this technique at various angles to build the crown of petals.

Second: Leaves Fill a medium-size paper cone with lavender royal icing and a #352 leaf tip. Position the open side of the tip at a 45° angle. Apply a burst of pressure and leave the tip in place for a few seconds to build up the head of the leaf and then pull the tip toward you. Stop the pressure. Pipe leaves in the negative spacing between the sweet pea clusters.

Third: Plunger Flowers This flower is discussed in Chapter 6 and used in many chapters of this book. Once you review the section on making plunger flowers (see page 100), position mauve plunger flowers in the negative spacing not filled in by the leaves for a more compact and fuller look.

Fourth: Dots Fill a small paper cone with moss-green royal icing and a PME #0 tip. Pipe dots under the crown of petals, in clusters of six or more dots, for a more complete look.

Piping the first petals for sweet pea clusters.

Adding leaves to the sweet pea clusters.

PASTILLAGE DISKS

Trace the pattern for the crown of disks that surrounds the second tier of this cake (see page 256) or use a 1½-in. (3.8 cm) round cookie cutter.

First, dust a work surface with a light coating of cornstarch and use a nonstick rolling pin to roll out pastillage paste very thin. Cut out as many disks as you can with a round cookie cutter. Before the disks dry, cut out a small triangle from each of the disks or use the pattern as a guide to cut the triangle. This

negative space is where you will attach the disk to the shoulder of the cake. Let the disks dry overnight.

When ready to attach, pipe moss-green royal icing into the cavity of the disks and carefully attach the disks to the shoulder of the cake.

Hold the first disk in place for 20 to 30 seconds to ensure that it adheres to the cake. The next disk should be about ½ to ¾ in. (1.3 to 1.9 cm) apart. Continue until you have gone completely around the cake. Pipe dots in clusters between the disks as you did under the crown of petals.

Adding royal icing to a pastillage disk.

Attaching a pastillage disk to the cake shoulder.

Adding more pastillage disks to the cake.

TRELLIS (DROP STRING)

Load a medium-size paper cone with pinkish Egg White Royal Icing and a PME #0 tip. Start under the disk, about ½ in. (1.3 cm) away from the cake. Apply light pressure as you touch the disk. Then apply more pressure as you pull the string toward yourself—1½ to 2 in. (3.8 to 5.1 cm) long. Then skip over the next disk and attach the string to the third disk.

For the next trellis, reposition the tip where you just left off and connect another trellis—skipping over the next disk and connecting to the following one. Continue until you have gone completely around the cake. Let dry for 10 or more minutes.

CONNECTING TRELLIS

Position the #0 tip at the center point of one of the trellises. Apply a small burst of pressure from the paper cone and allow the icing to expel from the tip. Touch the trellis (with the icing only) and pull the icing about 1½ to 2 in. (3.8 to 5.1 cm) long and then carefully attach the icing to the center point of the next trellis. Continue with this technique until you have gone completely around the cake.

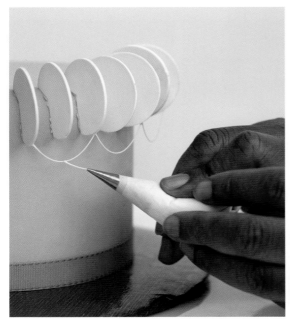

Piping trellis work on the bottoms of the pastillage disks.

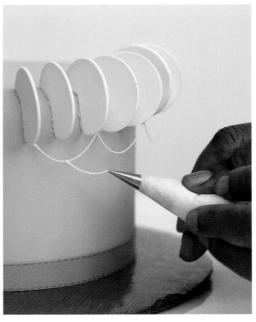

Connecting the trellis work.

BAND OF TRELLIS WORK

Pipe a band of trellis work around the top center of the pastillage disks, skipping over every other disk, for a more complete look.

APPLIQUÉ FLOWERS

Rub a tiny amount of white vegetable shortening on a work surface and use a nonstick rolling pin to roll out 2 oz (57 g) gumpaste in pink and lavender tones. Cut out various blossoms and attach to the bottom of the second tier. (See page 104 for more details on appliqué work.)

OVERPIPING

The top of the bottom tier has intricate overpiping work, as explained and discussed in Chapter 6 (see page 98). Once the cake has been measured, start with the top row and a #3 round tip. Place an object under the cake to give you a better position in piping or use a tilting turntable to tilt the cake when piping. Pipe the first scallop around the cake and immediately pipe another line directly on top. Allow to dry for 10 minutes. Then overpipe the line again. Then pipe the next scallop line under the overpiped line with a distance of ⅛ to ¼ in. (3 to 6 mm) between the two lines. Overpipe it once. Then pipe a third scallop line under the second overpipe line with a distance of ⅛ to ¼ in. (3 to 6 mm) between them. Do not overpipe this line. Finally, switch to a #0 tip or a #1 tip and pipe a fourth scallop line with no overpiping.

Piping trellis work around the middles of the pastillage disks.

cake 2

PEACHES AND CREAM CAKE

This is a three-tier cake with floral stencils on each tier. The top and bottom tiers are covered with cream rolled fondant, and the middle tier is covered with peach rolled fondant. The sides of each tier are decorated with a floral stencil.

The top tier is decorated with white chocolate roses in peach and a yellow/cream color and green foliage, and the finale is a ribbon bouquet with peach petals at the bottom of the second tier.

The cake rests on a simple cream-colored round drum.

Hold the bud in your nonwriting hand and one of the shaped petals in your writing hand. Place the center of the shaped petal at the seam of the bud. The height of the petal should be the same as or slightly greater than that of the bud. Press the petal to the cone until it sticks. Pull down on the heavy part of the petal so it shapes to the cone. Next, move the petal counterclockwise to the right of the previous petal; then move it back about one-third of the distance of the attached petal. Attach the next petal the same way, but this time the fourth petal should go inside the flap of the second petal. The rosebud is complete.

Medium-Size Roses

Shape five more balls of White Modeling Chocolate Paste. Flatten and shape each ball into a rose petal as just described.

Pick up the rosebud in your nonwriting hand and one of the shaped petals in your writing hand. Place the petal slightly to the left or right of one of the rosebud seams. The new shaped petals should be the same height as the previous petals or slightly higher. Attach the petals in a counter-clockwise direction (for right-handers) or clockwise direction (for left-handers).

Push the petal to the rosebud and pull down on the heavy part to shape it to the bud. Do not seal the seams of the petals when they are attached. Pick up the second shaped petal and move the petal counterclockwise to the right of the previous petal; then move it back about one-third of the distance of the attached petal. Attach the second petal to the first petal. Pull down on the heavy part of the petal to shape it to the rosebud. Do not seal in the seams.

Continue with the next two shaped petals in the same fashion. When attaching the fifth and final petal, lap the petal over the fourth attached petal. Lift up the first

petal and tuck the fifth petal inside it. Lap the first petal over the fifth. Go back and look over each petal. To reshape, use your index finger to push the center point of each petal forward and then pinch the petal with your thumb and index finger. The medium-size rose is complete.

To petal-dust, choose colors that are slightly darker than the flowers and colors that are much deeper. First, petal-dust with the slightly darker shades over each of the petals and then use the much deeper shades only on the edges of each petal. Dust the centers with the deepest shades.

Adding petals to a cone foundation to form a medium-size hand-shaped rose with a total of nine petals.

STENCILS

Rebeat about 4 ounces (114 g) of Meringue Powder Royal Icing in a small metal bowl using an offset metal spatula. Add 1 tsp (5 ml) cold water to thin the icing. Carefully attach a stencil of your choice to the cake with masking tape. Load the offset spatula with icing and carefully spread the icing over the stencil in one even and swift motion. You might need to go back over the stencil to make sure you have covered every cavity in the stencil. Carefully remove the stencil.

STENCILING ON A ROUND CAKE

It is rare to find a stencil pattern that goes completely around a cake, which makes it easier to stencil a cake. Thus, you need to apply the stencil pattern in stages. After attaching the stencil to the cake and icing the stencil with royal icing, carefully remove the stencil without disturbing the shape of the pattern. Allow the first stenciled pattern to dry for 15 to 20 minutes before you reattach the stencil on an unstenciled side of the cake.

To make the pattern look continuous (as if you had used one large stencil to go completely around the cake), pipe some freehand embroidery piping between the stencils, or just stencil a small section of the pattern in the spaces between each stenciled pattern.

Spreading royal icing on a stencil.

Lifting the stencil to reveal the design underneath.

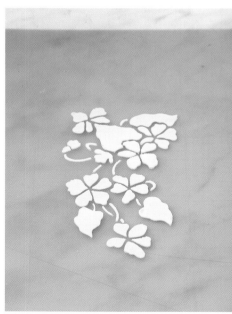

The complete stenciled design.

cake 3

CASCADE RIBBON CAKE

This simple wedding cake is a four-tier monochromatic cake enrobed in a mauve rolled fondant. On the top tier is a textured ribbon spray made of gumpaste with gumpaste ribbons cascading from the top to the bottom tier. Each tier is decorated with Swiss dots.

how-to techniques

CASCADE RIBBONS

Rub a tiny amount of white vegetable shortening on a work surface and use a nonstick rolling pin to roll out 4 oz (114 g) gumpaste to ¼ in. (6 mm) thin. Texture it with a silk-textured rolling pin or a textured pin of your choice. Cut out strips 8 to 10 in. (20.3 to 25.4 cm) long and 1½ to 2 in. (3.8 to 5.1 cm) wide. Attach the strips to the top of the cake and let the strips cascade down the cake.

RIBBON BOUQUET

See the instructions for ribbon loops in Chapter 2 (see pages 26 and 30).

The ribbon loops on this cake are about 4 in. (10.2 cm) long and 1½ to 2 in. (3.8 to 5.1 cm) wide. The ribbons are textured with a silk-textured rolling pin, and the loops are glued together with pasteurized egg white.

Once the ribbon loops are dried, take a walnut-sized amount of commercial rolled fondant and place it in the center of the cake. Glue the fondant with a dab of Meringue Powder Royal Icing.

Attach the loops around the fondant, keeping the loops as close to each other as possible. Then place another piece of fondant on top of the bow and assemble the remaining bows on top.

textile-inspired designs

Hot colors make these dazzling wedding cakes extra special. Textile-inspired red circles, bubble-wrap texture, tassels, and textured leaves give a feeling of dimension, while a red hibiscus flower adds a subtle sensuality. Drawing inspiration from the look and textures of different fabrics, the cake artist can create stylish designs for any couple.

the couple

Elizabeth and Bobby met at an ice hockey game. Elizabeth's nephew is a member of the hockey team, and Bob is coach for these six-year-olds. Bob asked her out for a cappuccino after each game, and their relationship started to blossom.

Elizabeth works for a family business that runs a textile operation. When she is not at the family business, she drives a school bus that takes emotionally challenged children from their homes to school. She also takes her nephew Justin to his ice hockey games.

Bob is a park ranger and enjoys the outdoors as well as outdoor sports. He is an expert on various types of trees and foliage, and in his spare time he coaches ice hockey.

This Philadelphia couple is bursting with love for each other and for the people around them. They are looking for that perfect wedding that symbolizes their love and devotion to each other.

the consultation

The cake artist wanted to pull in both Bob and Elizabeth's interests in designing the cake. After looking through pictures and books and sampling cakes and icings, the couple couldn't decide on what they wanted. So the cake artist decided to pull in their careers as a basis for creating some quick sketches.

elements of the cake

The couple has decided on the Red Velvet Cake with a Cream Cheese Buttercream icing as a filling and as the icing under the Rolled Fondant. The first sketch is made up of 6-, 8-, and 10-in. (15.2, 20.3, and 25.4 cm) rounds. The bottom tier is 1½ in. (3.8 cm) tall. The cake serves 75 to 80 guests. The second sketch is made up of 6- and 8-in. (15.2 and 20.3 cm) rounds and serves 40 to 45 guests.

development of the cake designs

The cake artist uses the sketches to come up with creative designs for the couple. The following two cakes represent the cake artist's creativity during the development process:

CAKE 1: *Red and White Cake*

In this sketch the cake artist is thinking bold. The top and bottom tiers are red, and the middle tier is white. There is some type of texture on the bottom tier and red circles on the middle tier, along with some cornelli lace piping, which ties into Elizabeth's work with textiles.

CAKE 2: *Maple Leaf and Tassel Cake*

The cake artist sketches a two-tier cake all in white with brown drapery around the middle of the cake. The cake artist is thinking of a foliage design to bring in Bob's career and interests.

cake 1

RED AND WHITE CAKE

This striking cake has 2½ tiers and is enrobed in red and white. The top and bottom tiers are covered in red rolled fondant, and the middle tier is covered in white rolled fondant. On the top tier are gumpaste handmade hibiscus and red tulle. The middle tier has red circles in different sizes, including some smaller circles on top of larger circles. There is some freehand cornelli lace piping between some of the circles.

The bottom tier is textured to look like a piece of textile and resembles bubble wrap. The top edge of this bottom tier is decorated with red lace for a final finish.

how-to techniques

HIBISCUS

Start by making the pistil of the flower. The pistil is the center of the hibiscus. To make the pistil, shape ½ oz (14 g) of the red gum-paste into a log about 2 in. (5.1 cm) long. Roll the paste in the center with the back of a paintbrush or a modeling stick to form a waist. Dip 1 in. (2.5 cm) of 24-gauge wire into egg white and ease it up the pistil and through the waist. Pinch the paste to secure it to the wire. With angled tweezers, make five ridges at the bottom of the pistil. Distribute the ridges evenly,

making them between ¼ and ½ in. (6 mm and 1.3 cm) long.

Make the stigma by placing five ¼-in. (6 mm) stamens on top of the pistil. The stamens should have heads, which you will pollinate later with cornmeal. Cut five plastic sta-mens and place them symmetrically around the top of the pistil. Cut the remaining stamens (without heads) into ¼-in. (6 mm) pieces for a to-tal of 30 to 40 stamens. Randomly attach the stamens at a 45° angle to the upper portion of the pistil, above the waist. Let dry for several hours or overnight.

For the petals, roll ½ oz (14 g) of red paste into a log about 3 in. (7.6 cm) long. Dip a 24-gauge wire in egg white and insert it about ½ in. (1.3 cm) into the end of the log. Pinch the log to secure it to the wire. Place the wired log on a work surface rubbed with a tiny amount of white vegetable shortening and flatten the center of the log with a nonstick rolling pin. Roll the paste on either side of the centered wire with a modeling stick. This is the same procedure you used for mak-ing the tiger lily (see page 126).

Dust a clean area of the work surface with a light coating of

From top to bottom: Rolling the gumpaste for the pistil, wiring the pistil, and adding the stamens.

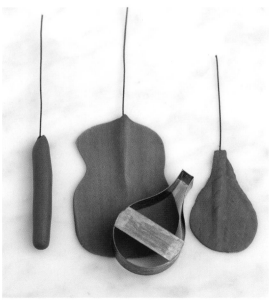

From left to right: Rolling and wiring a gumpaste log, stretching the gumpaste, and cutting with a metal cutter to form a hibiscus petal.

cornstarch and place the wired paste on it. Cut out the petal with a hibiscus cutter. Remove the excess paste and wrap tightly in plastic wrap. Firmly press the petal in a large leaf press. Remove the embossed petal and place it on a cell pad. Soften and ruffle the edges of the petal with a dogbone tool. Drape the petal over a rolling pin to dry in a natural curve. Using the same procedure, make four more petals. Let the five petals dry overnight on the rolling pin.

Petal-dust with a deeper shade of red petal dust, starting at the base of the petal and moving the color up the center of the petal. Petal-dust the edge of the flower with a much deeper red, such as a dogwood rose color or even a violet color. Petal-dust the pistil near the bottom with the red petal dust and then go over the very bottom with the deeper red color.

When ready to assemble, arrange each petal between the ridges at the bottom of the pistil. Start with two to three petals, making sure the end of each is directly between two ridges. Tape the petals securely with florist tape. Add the balance of the petals to the pistil and retape the entire flower.

TEXTILE BUBBLE WRAP

Roll out red fondant ¼ to ½ in. (6 mm to 1.3 cm) thick on a surface dusted lightly with cornstarch. Use a rolling pin with a textured design to roll out the paste exactly the same way as was done in Chapter 2 (see page 23).

RED CIRCLES

Roll out red rolled fondant about ⅛ in. (3 mm) thick on a surface lightly dusted with cornstarch. Cut out circles with small cookie cutters, ranging in size from ¼ to ½ in. (6 mm to 1.3 cm). Attach with water to the cake.

Texturing and shaping a hibiscus petal.

A completed hibiscus with five ruffled petals and a center pistil.

MAPLE LEAF AND TASSEL CAKE

This is a small two-tier cake enrobed in white rolled icing. This cake has a fall/winter theme. Both tiers are decorated with layers upon layers of chocolate maple leaves, along with freehand drapery, gumpaste streamers, and gold tassels.

The top tier is decorated with chocolate drop stringwork and fine cornelli lace pipework, and the bottom tier is decorated with cornelli lace and freehand embroidery piping. The top tier is decorated with a spray of maple leaves and tassels.

how-to techniques

TASSELS

Knead about 1 oz (28 g) of gold-colored rolled fondant with a little vegetable shortening. Shape it into a 2-in. (5.1 cm) log. Place the log into a clay gun fitted with a wire-mesh multihole disk. Place the plunger into the gun and apply a lot of pressure as the spaghetti-like strings start to emerge from the gun. Continue to squeeze until about 1½ in. (5.1 cm) of paste emerges from the gun. Cut with an X-acto knife.

Continue with the same technique to make more tassels.

A clay gun, which is used in making tassels.

Pushing colored rolled fondant through a clay gun.

Cutting tassels from the clay gun.

Pinching the ends of the tassels for a finished look.

MAPLE LEAF

Rub a tiny amount of white vegetable shortening on a work surface and use a nonstick rolling pin to roll out chocolate-colored commercial rolled fondant about 1/16 in. (1.5 mm) thick. Dust a clean area of the work surface with a light coating of cornstarch and place the fondant on it. Cut out as many leaves as possible with a maple leaf cutter. Emboss the leaves with a leaf press to give texture and soften the edges of the leaves with a dogbone tool. Attach to the cake with water or pasteurized egg white.

FREEHAND DRAPERY

Knead 8 oz (228 g) of commercial rolled fondant or gumpaste until it is pliable. Sprinkle the work surface lightly with cornstarch and use a nonstick rolling pin to roll out the paste into a loose rectangle, about 6 × 9 in. (15.2 × 22.9 cm) and 1/8 to 1/4 in. (3 to 6 mm) thick. Square off the paste.

With a pastry brush and a little water, brush the area of the cake where the drapery will be placed. Fold under the top and bottom edges of the paste about 1/2 in. (1.3 cm) in to form a finished edge for your drape (see photos on page 116).

Pick up one end of the drape and gently gather it into soft folds. Then pick up the other end of the drape and do the same. Gently pick up the paste and pull it until it forms drapes. Carefully attach the drape to the damp area on the cake. Taper the ends of the paste and tear off any excess. See Chapters 6 and 7 for additional instructions on freehand drapery.

CHAPTER TWELVE

setting up a cake design business

Cake decorating is an exciting enterprise. It can be a rewarding part-time or serious full-time business. Anyone who decorates cakes for family or friends or for profit can tell you that the reward of executing something well is almost as important as what you get for it. Cake decorating is a labor of love and combines baking and fine art in a way that continues to astonish admirers. But anyone who is seriously considering it as a business should be aware of some pros and cons to putting an establishment together.

Before you even begin to plan a business, there is a lot to consider. Can you afford to go weeks or months without income when business is slow? Are you willing to be "married" to the business 24-7? And, finally, do you have the support of your family and/or business partners or investors?

If you can say yes to most of these questions, you have what it takes to make it in this challenging but rewarding business.

HOME BASE vs. RENTING OR LEASING SPACE

f you are making only a few cakes a week, renting or leasing professional space can be an expensive proposition, especially if you don't have regular business or a location that might give you retail traffic. Almost all cake designers work by appointment. The "shop" or "kitchen" is not retail oriented. Thus, there are no muffins, scones, cakes, cookies, or pies ready to be sold to customers passing by. There are, however, cafés and specialty shops such as "Cupcake Café," "Magnolia," "Betty Bakery," "Elaine's," and others that do custom design work, plus they have retail establishments. These establishments usually have a lot of employees, versus the independent cake artist that may run the business with as little as one person. Most states won't allow you to bake, decorate, and sell cakes for profit from your home kitchen. If you do, you are breaking the law. If you sell a cake once in a while, and you don't advertise commercially, some states might not consider what you're doing a "business" according to the law. You might be able to work from your home kitchen in this limited way, provided you contact the department of health in your area. Baking in some states may fall under the department of agriculture. In this instance, it may be OK for you to bake at home, provided you follow all of the rules. It becomes a problem, however, when you start growing and doing more business and are still working from your home kitchen. In cases where you still can't afford to rent or lease, you might consider contacting your local church, synagogue, or local club or facility that has a licensed kitchen, which has already been inspected by the health department and carries liability coverage. You might be able to use these facilities until you are ready to rent or lease space. In any event, you should at least carry product liability insurance in case someone gets sick from eating your goods. This will be discussed in more detail later in this chapter. For more information and answers on setting up a home-based business, and the requirements for your state, visit www.powerhomebiz.com.

If you own your home and you have a basement with a separate entrance or a converted garage with a separate entrance, you may be eligible for commercial space conversion. It all depends on the state where you live, the rules for that state, and the local zoning laws. Finally, you may also wish to look into commercial kitchen rentals. This might be an affordable option when you have a big order or if your work is sporadic. The following website will assist you in finding kitchen space within a certain distance from your zip code: www.commercialkitchen-forrent.com.

PING YOUR BUSINESS

OAT

nderstand that a cake
design business oper-
ates differently from
a bakery. Cake studios
lly have walk-in traffic.
s done by appointment.
this way because these
ot selling day-to-day
-in customers. You
a good volume of busi-
n operation or have
lientele: day-to-day
om you are produc-
ed and decorated
entele that can afford
cakes that are made
might also need to
other things to keep
afloat when high-end
aren't coming in, such
muffins, scones, deco-
s, brownies, and other
ll items. These items
high priced and can
d returns when sold
specially during slow
year.

Establishing a good rapport
with high-end retailers in your
area can be extremely profitable.
Most retailers purchase baked
goods from local sources (which
can include you). Of course, these
goods must be priced on the low-
end side to be attractive to the
high-end retailer. The lower your
prices, the more they buy from
you, and the more you sell, the
more you make.

You may wish to consider go-
ing into business with a partner or
sharing a leased or rented space
and running your own separate
business. This type of shared space
can greatly reduce the cost of rent
and utilities. But before you consider this, make sure you can live
with the person you are sharing
space with.

WHAT IS YOUR STYLE OF CAKE ART?

t is important to know what type of designer you wish to be or the type of clients you wish to attract. Your style of work will dictate what category you may fall into, such as whimsical, character, theme, classical, or perhaps all four. This can be an important factor in attracting a specific type of clientele. If you live near a lot of schools or in a community where there are lots of children, there are plenty of opportunities for you to design birthday cakes. It might be wise to put on your "character or theme" hat to attract that specific group. Designing three-dimensional cake sculptures of puppets or animals could bring in a lot more bucks than just making simply iced cakes with piped top and bottom borders, a few piped flowers, and a birthday greeting. But remember, those simply iced cakes can bring in a lot of business when there are no upscale cakes on order. Moreover, if you live in an area where people can afford pricey items, a beautiful cake covered in rolled fondant with some delicate pipework and a spray of gumpaste flowers might open their eyes and their wallets. Wherever you are, you need to design your business to attract the clientele you seek.

DEVELOPING YOUR STYLE OF CAKE ART

It may be difficult in the beginning to put your cake decorating skills in a style category. Generally, the customers you attract and the type of cakes they order will determine how comfortable you are in doing a specific "style" of decorating. The orders you get may vary according to your location, the people who know you, and the prices of your cakes. Most American cake artists start out making simple cakes with buttercream icing and buttercream pipework. As they gain confidence and take a few more classes, they branch out into using rolled fondant, royal icing work, and gumpaste flowers. Slowly, the cake artist develops a name and a style that is associated with the type of work he or she does.

EQUIPMENT NEEDS

You need equipment. If you rent commercial space by the hour, the kitchen will probably be equipped with all you need. If you are using space from a local community club, you may need to bring in additional equipment. If you are renting or leasing your own space, you need to outfit it. If this is a small space, then the space will dictate what you can have in it, but at the very least you will need an oven, a work surface, and a range of baking ingredients and decorating tools.

Large Equipment

WORK BENCH: Your work bench could be made up of one or two 8 × 2-ft. (2.4 × 0.61 m) wood counters with aluminum bottom shelves. If you put two tables together, you have a wide space to work from, especially if you are icing and covering cakes in rolled fondant. To cover the seam where the two tables meet and achieve a surface area of 8 × 4 ft (2.4 × 1.2 m), you can purchase a piece of kitchen counter material to fit the top surface of both tables. These can be purchased and cut to size from Home Depot or Lowe's.

OVENS: You will need a heavy-duty oven or a single or double convection oven. To save money, research restaurant equipment suppliers in your area to find a refurbished oven with a service contract. Brand-new ovens are expensive. You might also wish to consider one or two induction stovetop units. These are great if you don't have a traditional stovetop burner, and they can be put away easily.

REFRIGERATION: You will need a large commercial refrigerator as well as a separate freezer with thermometers.

SINKS: You will need to have both a three-compartment sink with a grease trap installed and a hand sink.

HEATING AND AIR-CONDITIONING: Air-conditioning is important, especially when the weather is extremely hot and humid.

Buttercream-iced cakes can be refrigerated, but rolled fondant–iced cakes should not be refrigerated unless you have a special refrigerator where you can zero out the humidity. Rolled fondant–iced cakes can be left out at room temperature for up to 2 days if the temperature of your facility is kept at 65° to 68°F (18° to 20°C). You should be mindful as to the type of filling used inside cakes with rolled icing. A preserved filling is less perishable than a curd filling.

COOLING RACKS: You should have one or two large cooling racks with wheels.

STORAGE: You will need shelving for ingredients, pans, and the like, as well as a storage case for all of your artistry tools and equipment.

MIXERS: If you are making birthday, celebration, or wedding cakes, it might be smart to purchase a 20-quart Hobart mixer for heavy-duty work and one or two 5- or 6-quart mixers for smaller jobs.

Small Equipment

- Baking pans in different sizes and shapes
- Stainless-steel turntables
- Large containers for holding ingredients
- A microwave oven
- Cardboard rounds and squares
- Foam core
- Masonite rounds and squares (for heavy-duty cakes)
- Styrofoam
- Cake foil
- Masking tape
- Boxes
- Rubber spatulas and offset metal spatulas
- Handheld wire whisks
- Metal bowls
- Measuring cups and spoons and liquid measuring cups
- A good electronic scale that measures in grams, ounces, milliliters, kilograms, and fluid ounces
- Nonstick or wood rolling pins

Baking Ingredients

- All-purpose flour
- Cake flour
- Granulated sugar
- Confectioners' sugar
- Spices
- Cocoa powder
- Baking powder
- Baking soda
- Salt
- Corn syrup
- Cornstarch
- Vegetable and high-ratio shortenings
- Extracts and oils
- Gel and paste food coloring

RECOMMENDED SIZES

BAKING PANS 6 x 2 in. (15.2 x 5.1 cm) to 18 x 2 in. (45.7 x 5.1 cm)

CARDBOARD ROUNDS AND SQUARES: 6 to 22 in. (15.2 to 55.9 cm)

BOXES: 6 to 22 in. (15.2 to 55.9 cm)

METAL BOWLS: small, medium, large, very large, or 6 to 22 in. (15.2 to 55.9 cm)

PLASTIC CONTAINERS: half pint, pint, and quart sizes, or 8 oz (228 g or 240 ml), 16 oz (454 g or 473 ml), and 32 oz (907 g or 946 ml)

LARGE CONTAINERS: heavy-duty bins to accommodate 50 to 100 lb (22.7 to 45.4 kg) of cake flour, all-purpose flour, granulated sugar, and confectioners' sugar

Cake Artistry Tools

- Florist wires in different gauges
- Petal dust
- Veiners
- Leaf presses
- Gumpaste cutters
- Modeling tools
- Palette and X-acto knives
- Small nonstick rolling pins
- Vegetable gums
- Cell pads
- Rounded toothpicks

There are many sources where you can purchase these items. A few of the best sources for baking and decorating equipment include www.cakedeco.com, www.ckproducts.com, www.beryls.com, and www.nycake.com.

THE LEGAL SIDE OF THINGS

If you are operating this business alone, you can obtain a license as a sole proprietorship. If you have a name for your business and you are sure that the name does not exist elsewhere, you can register your business name with your local county clerk's office. There you will receive your business certificate. Next, you can fill out an SS-4 form (Employers' Identification Number) from the IRS and get a tax ID number for your business name. Once you receive this, you can go to any commercial bank and open up a commercial checking account with your business name. This number is also important when you wish to purchase supplies and equipment for your business. With this ID number, you can purchase your items at wholesale prices and without tax. You can get your tax ID number online at www.gov-tax.com/taxid/taxid_l.php?rdir=1226287438. You should also obtain a food safety license or a serve/safe license. This is done by passing a course, which can be taken online at www.serve-safe.com. Next, you should get your establishment inspected by the department of health, which, if you pass, will issue you a health inspection license.

You also need to purchase general liability insurance. This is important in case someone falls and gets hurt on the doorsteps of your business or a cake collapses or something breaks during delivery. You should also purchase product liability insurance, just in case someone is harmed from eating your baked goods. If this is a home-based business, you can get a rider attached to your homeowner's or renter's insurance for the full value of your equipment. If this is not a home-based business, you should have both product and general liability insurance coverage. You may also wish to consider business interruption insurance in case of a catastrophe. This will cover rent, utilities, and salaries. If you grow and add employees to your business, you will need to add workers' compensation insurance.

ESTABLISHING YOURSELF

nitially, getting yourself established is hard work. Getting work from friends, family, and community is a good way to help get you up and running, but it may not be enough. You should have clients that you have done work for before you open your business. This includes individuals, party planners, catering halls, social clubs, churches, synagogues, theater groups, and corporations.

You may also need to do free work to help get your name out there. Presenting a free cake to your local firehouse, senior citizen center, a museum, or an auction house is a great way to tell people who you are and the type of cakes and artistry you offer. Even if these establishments don't actually get you a cake order, they might recommend you.

Getting a website is also essential in promoting and selling your business. It provides the future customer a look into your world and what type of services you provide. Your website should reflect your personality and your style of work. It should be engaging, easy to navigate, and colorful yet tasteful and beautifully designed. If you sell merchandise, this can be placed on your site and you can sell directly from your site.

As your business grows, you will need help. One source of great help without the expenses associated with hiring employees is interns from culinary schools. Students majoring in pastry and baking generally need to do some type of externship before they can get their diploma. Many students want to focus on doing wedding cakes and specialty cakes as a career, and they are looking for people with this type of expertise to work for and learn from. As your business grows and achieves success, the world will know who you are. Certainly, culinary schools will also have an interest in you. But you don't have to wait until you are a "big wheel." You can call culinary schools in your area and let them know that you are interested in seeing their students for the possibility of an internship.

Last, getting your work published is a great way of expanding your business and your reputation. Several national magazines, such as *Brides, Modern Bride, InStyle, American Cake Decorating,* and *Pastry Art & Design,* are great outlets for presenting your work to the world. Call and ask for an appointment to see the editor. Make sure you bring a portfolio of your work. Most of the photos can be taken with a 35 mm camera, but you want one or two of the photos taken by a professional food photographer.

NETWORKING

Joining organizations that specialize in cake decorating is a wonderful resource for you. You can keep abreast of the latest in cake decorating ideas and techniques and learn where to purchase new and exciting tools for your art. Some of these organizations will list the names of noted cake artists who are traveling and teaching classes in various states. These learning opportunities are invaluable, as you always want to perfect your skills and acquire new ones. Many of these organizations have monthly publications. Some show pictures of cakes from conventions from cake artists around the globe and how they were created, including recipes and techniques. Some organizations may have "days of sharing" in your local area where you can get together with others who share your passion and business. There you can take mini-classes or watch demonstrations by noted cake artists and network with people around you. Here are a few organizations you may want to consider joining:

THE INTERNATIONAL CAKE EXPLORATION SOCIETÉ (ICES)

www.ices.org

This is a wonderful organization to begin with. The dues are $60 a year, and with that you get a monthly magazine. Part of your dues goes to your local state chapter. Each state or country has a local ICES representative. They will get in touch with you to invite you to local days of sharing.

CAKE DECORATING MEET-UP

www.cakedecorating.meetup.com

This site allows you to type in your zip code and find a club or group of other individuals who share your passion and interest.

BAKER'S DOZEN

www.bakersdozen.org

This is a great organization of amateur and professional bakers and cake decorators. The fees are nominal, and the organization is represented by cities in three states: San Francisco, New York, and Salt Lake City.

There are also several magazines that you should consider subscribing to:

- *American Cake Decorating* magazine is a great source of information for amateurs and professionals alike, with wonderful pictures and articles. (www.americancakedecorating.com)

- *Cake Craft and Decoration* is a lovely magazine with lots of projects in each issue. (www.cake-craft.com)

- *Cakes & Sugarcraft* is a cake decorating magazine from the UK. (www.cakesandsugarcraft.co.uk/home)

And finally, there are several chat lines that can really be of service to you in your search for recipes and to help you solve problems with icings, transporting cakes, or just about anything you can think of. One such chat line is www.cakecentral.com.

CHAPTER THIRTEEN

recipes and flavor combinations

These recipes and flavor combinations are from a collection of recipes I have acquired, tweaked, and developed over the past three decades. They represent great taste and flavors and some are from my grandmother's kitchen. I was inspired to bake after watching her make cakes from scratch using a wooden spoon, a large bowl, and a handful of this and a handful of that! Enjoy!

RECIPES

chocolate pound cake

EQUIPMENT: *5- or 6-quart mixer*

YIELD: *two 9-in. (22.9 cm) cakes*

BAKING TIME: *30 to 35 minutes*

12 oz (340 g) cake flour

1 lb (454 g) granulated sugar

1 tsp (4 g) baking soda

5 Tbsp (40 g) cocoa powder

1 tsp (5 g) salt

12 oz (340 g) unsalted butter, half completely melted

3 fl oz (89 ml or 85 g) whole milk

5 large eggs

10 fl oz (296 ml or 283 g) buttermilk

2 Tbsp (30 ml) chocolate extract

Preheat the oven to 325°F (163°C). Vegetable-spray and parchment-line the cake pans.

Sift together the cake flour, sugar, baking soda, cocoa powder, and salt. Add the butter and mix for 3 minutes on low speed. Then mix on the next-higher speed for 1 minute. Check to make sure there are no lumps of butter still in the batter. Add the whole milk and mix for 3 minutes on low speed. Then mix on the next-higher speed for 1 minute.

Whisk the eggs, buttermilk, and chocolate extract together. Add the egg mixture to the batter in four increments.

Pour the batter into the prepared pans and bake until a toothpick inserted in the center comes out clean.

lemon pound cake

EQUIPMENT: *5- or 6-quart mixer or 20-quart Hobart*

YIELD: *one 10 ×3-in. (25.4 ×7.6 cm) cake or two 8-in. (20.3 cm) cakes*

BAKING TIME: *95 minutes for a 10 ×3-in. (25.4 ×7.6 cm) cake pan, 30 to 35 minutes for 8-in. (20.3 cm) cake pans*

1 lb (454 g) cake flour

1 lb (454 g) granulated sugar

1½ Tbsp (18 g) baking powder

1 tsp (5 g) salt

8 oz (227 g) unsalted butter, softened

8 oz (227 g) cream cheese, softened

2 Tbsp (30 ml or 28 g) fresh lemon juice

Grated zest of 3 lemons

4 oz (114 g) Lemon Curd (page 23)

5 large eggs

8 fl oz (237 ml or 227 g) whole milk

Preheat the oven to 350°F (177°C). Vegetable-spray and parchment-line the cake pans.

Mix the flour, sugar, baking powder, and salt in a large bowl. Mix for 2 minutes on stir speed with the paddle attachment to sift and blend the ingredients.

Add the butter, cream cheese, lemon juice, zest, and lemon curd and beat on low speed for 1 minute. Stop and scrape the bowl. Beat for 2 minutes on medium-high speed. Stop and scrape the bowl. Beat for another minute.

Whisk the eggs and whole milk together. Add to the batter in 3 increments on low speed. Stop and scrape the bowl; then increase the speed to medium and beat for 2 minutes. Stop, scrape the bowl, and then beat for 1 minute longer.

Pour the batter into the prepared pans and bake until a toothpick inserted in the center comes out clean.

NOTE: This recipe may be multiplied several times.

red velvet cake

EQUIPMENT: *5- or 6-quart mixer*

YIELD: *two 10-in. (25.4 cm) cakes*

BAKING TIME: *75 to 85 minutes*

12 oz (340 g) cake flour

1½ lb (682 g) granulated sugar

1 tsp (4 g) baking powder

4 Tbsp (32 g) dark cocoa powder

½ tsp (2.5 g) salt

12 oz (340 g) unsalted butter, half completely melted

2 fl oz (59 ml or 57 g) whole milk

6 eggs

8 fl oz (237 ml or 227 g) buttermilk

1 tsp (5 ml or 2 g) vanilla extract

2 Tbsp (1 oz or 28 g) red food coloring

Preheat the oven to 325°F (163°C). Vegetable-spray and parchment-line the cake pans.

Sift together the flour, sugar, baking powder, cocoa powder, and salt. Add the butter and mix for 3 minutes on low speed. Then mix on the next-higher speed for 1 minute. Check to make sure there are no lumps of butter still in the batter. The batter will look coarse and crumbly. Add the whole milk and mix for 3 minutes on low speed. Then mix on the next-higher speed for 1 minute.

Whisk the eggs, buttermilk, vanilla, and red food coloring together. Add the egg mixture to the batter in four increments.

Pour the batter into the prepared pans and bake until a toothpick inserted into the center comes out clean.

NOTE: You can substitute corn or canola oil for the butter. Both oils produce a moist cake, but the cake rises higher when made with butter.

german chocolate cake

EQUIPMENT: *5- or 6-quart mixer*

YIELD: *two 9-in. (22.9 cm) cakes*

BAKING TIME: *35 to 40 minutes*

4 oz (114 g) unsweetened or bittersweet chocolate

4 fl oz (118 ml or 114 g) boiling water

1 tsp (5 ml or 2.5 g) vanilla extract

8 oz (227 g) butter, softened

1 lb (454 g) granulated sugar

4 eggs, separated

10 oz (283 g) cake flour

½ tsp (2.5 g) salt

1 tsp (4 g) baking soda

8 fl oz (237 ml or 227 g) buttermilk

Preheat the oven to 350°F (177°C). Vegetable-spray and parchment-line the cake pans.

Cut up the chocolate and place in a metal bowl. Add the boiling water and let sit until the chocolate dissolves — about 5 minutes. Whisk until the chocolate is smooth and cooled. Whisk in the vanilla and set aside.

Cream the butter and sugar together for 4 minutes. Stop and scrape the bowl. Then cream for another minute. Add the egg yolks, one at a time, until fully incorporated.

Slowly add the chocolate mixture to the creamed butter and sugar mixture.

Sift the cake flour, salt, and baking soda. Add this alternately with the buttermilk to the chocolate and butter mixture.

In a separate bowl, whisk the egg whites until they form medium to stiff peaks (about 5 minutes). Then carefully fold the whites into the batter until the whites disappear into the batter.

Pour the batter into the prepared cake pans and bake until a toothpick inserted in the center comes out clean.

NOTE: Recipe may be doubled or tripled.

almond paste cake

EQUIPMENT: *5- or 6-quart mixer*

Yield: two 7-in. (17.8 cm) cakes or one 10 × 3-in. (25.4 × 7.6 cm) cake

BAKING TIME: *45 minutes for 7-in. (17.8 cm) cake pans, 85 to 90 minutes for a 10 × 3-in. (25.4 × 7.6 cm) cake pan*

6 oz (170 g) unsalted butter, softened

4 oz (114 g) almond paste

1 tsp (5 ml or 2 g) vanilla extract

1 lb (454 g) granulated sugar

4 large eggs

10 oz (283 g) cake flour

1 Tbsp (12 g) baking powder

½ tsp (2.5 g) salt

8 fl oz (240 ml or 227 g) whole milk

Preheat the oven to 350°F (177°C). Vegetable-spray and parchment-line the cake pans.

Cream the butter, almond paste, vanilla, and sugar together for 4 minutes. Stop, scrape the bowl, and cream for another minute.

Add the eggs, one at a time, to the creamed mixture.

Sift together the flour, baking powder, and salt. Add the flour mixture and milk alternately to the creamed mixture. Pour the mixture into the baking pan. The batter will be thick.

Carefully smooth the batter with a metal offset spatula. Hit the pan against the counter to burst any air bubbles.

Bake until the cake shrinks slightly and a toothpick inserted in the center comes out clean.

dominican cake

EQUIPMENT: *5- or 6-quart mixer*

YIELD: *two 10-in. (25.4 cm) cakes*

BAKING TIME: *45 to 50 minutes*

1 lb (454 g) unsalted butter, softened

1 lb (454 g) granulated sugar

1 lb (454 g) cake flour

1 Tbsp (12 g) baking powder

¼ tsp (1.25 g) salt

2 Tbsp (16 g) cornstarch

8 fl oz (237 ml or 227 g) whole milk or pineapple juice

1 Tbsp (15 ml or 14 g) light rum

1 Tbsp (15 ml or 14 g) Dominican, Bourbon, or Madagascar vanilla extract

12 extra-large egg yolks

1 Tbsp (14 g) grated lemon zest

4 extra-large egg whites

Preheat the oven to 350°F (177°C). Vegetable-spray and parchment-line the cake pans.

Cream the butter on low speed for 2 minutes. Add all but 3 Tbsp (45 g) of the sugar and cream for 3 minutes. Stop, scrape the bowl, and cream for an additional 2 minutes. The mixture should be light and creamy.

In a separate bowl, mix the cake flour, baking powder, salt, and cornstarch. Sift the mixture twice. Meanwhile, in a separate bowl, mix the milk (or juice), rum, and vanilla together and set aside.

On low speed, add the egg yolks, one at a time, to the creamed butter and sugar mixture. Mix until the yolks disappear. Add the flour and liquid mixture alternately in three increments, starting with the flour. Add the lemon zest and mix for 30 seconds.

In a separate bowl, beat the egg whites until stiff (but not too dry), about 3 minutes on high speed. At the end of 2 minutes of beating, add the remaining 3 Tbsp (45 g) of sugar. Beat for another minute.

Carefully fold the egg whites into the cake batter. Pour the batter into the prepared pans (two-thirds full). Bake until the cake shrinks slightly from the pan and a toothpick inserted in the center comes out clean.

NOTE: Recipe may be doubled.

chocolate fudge cake

EQUIPMENT: *5- or 6-quart mixer*

YIELD: *two 8-in. (20.3 cm) cakes*

BAKING TIME: *45 to 50 minutes*

10 oz (283 g) all-purpose flour

10 oz (283 g) granulated sugar

6 oz (170 g) packed dark brown sugar

4 oz (114 g) Dutch process cocoa powder

2¼ tsp (9 g) baking soda

1½ tsp (7.5 g) salt

18 fl oz (532 ml or 510 g) buttermilk

8 oz (227 g) unsalted butter, half completely melted

2 large eggs

1½ tsp (7.5 ml) vanilla extract

6 oz (170 g) fine semisweet or bittersweet chocolate, melted

Preheat the oven to 350°F (177°C). Vegetable-spray and parchment-line the cake pans.

Measure all the ingredients except the chocolate into a large mixer bowl. Blend for 30 seconds on low speed, scraping the bowl constantly.

Blend in the melted chocolate and beat for 2 minutes on medium speed; then beat on high speed for 2 minutes, scraping the bowl. Note that lumps may appear in the batter due to the temperature of the butter. This is fine.

Pour the batter into the prepared pans and level them with a metal offset spatula.

Bake until a toothpick inserted in the center comes out clean. Cool the cakes in the pans and then turn out onto wire racks.

NOTE: This recipe may be multiplied several times.

carrot cake

EQUIPMENT: *5- or 6-quart mixer*

YIELD: *one 10 ×3-in. (25.4 ×7.6 cm) cake or two 9-in. (22.9 cm) cakes*

BAKING TIME: *90 minutes for a 10 ×3-in. (25.4 ×7.6 cm) cake pan, 55 to 60 minutes for 9-in. (22.9 cm) cake pans*

9 oz (255 g) all-purpose flour

1 lb (454 g) granulated sugar

2 tsp (8 g) baking soda

2 tsp (10 g) salt

2 tsp (3 g) ground cinnamon

12 fl oz (355 ml) vegetable, corn, or canola oil

4 large eggs

10 oz (283 g) grated carrot

5 oz (140 g) raisins

4 oz (114 g) chopped pecans

Preheat the oven to 350°F (177°C). Vegetable-spray and parchment-line the cake pans.

Mix the flour, sugar, baking soda, salt, and cinnamon for 2 minutes with the paddle attachment to sift the ingredients.

Add the oil and mix for 1 minute on low speed. Beat for 2 minutes on medium speed. Stop and scrape the bowl. Beat for another minute.

Whisk the eggs and add to the batter in two increments. Beat on medium-high speed for 3 minutes, until the batter turns light and golden. Stop and scrape the bowl. Beat for another minute.

Fold the carrot, raisins, and chopped pecans into the batter.

Pour the batter into the prepared pans and bake until a toothpick inserted in the center comes out clean. Cool in the pans for at least 15 to 20 minutes and then turn out onto cooling racks.

NOTE: This recipe may be multiplied several times.

almond/walnut pound cake

EQUIPMENT: *5- or 6-quart mixer*

YIELD: *two 10-in. (25.4 cm) cakes, three 9-in. (22.9 cm) cakes, or four 8-in. (20.3 cm) cakes*

BAKING TIME: *60 to 65 minutes for 10-in. (25.4 cm) cake pans, 55 to 60 minutes for 9-in. (22.9 cm) cake pans, 45 to 50 minutes for 8-in. (20.3 cm) cake pans*

1 lb (454 g) cake flour

1 lb (454 g) granulated sugar

1½ Tbsp (18 g) baking powder

1 tsp (5 g) salt

10 oz (283 g) unsalted butter, softened

6 oz (170 g) almond paste

2 fl oz (59 ml or 57 g) whole milk

4 large eggs

8 fl oz (236 ml or 227 g) buttermilk

2 tsp (10 ml) almond extract

6 oz (170 g) chopped walnuts

Preheat the oven to 350°F (177°C). Vegetable-spray and parchment-line the baking pans.

Mix the flour, sugar, baking powder, and salt with the paddle attachment for 3 minutes on stir speed.

Add the softened butter, almond paste, and whole milk. Beat on low speed for 2 minutes. Then beat on medium speed for 3 minutes.

Whisk the eggs, buttermilk, and extract together. Add to the batter in three increments on low speed. Beat on medium-high speed for 2 minutes.

Fold in the walnuts and pour into the prepared pans. Bake until a toothpick inserted in the center comes out clean.

lemon coconut cake

EQUIPMENT: *5- or 6-quart mixer*

YIELD: *two 8-in. (20.3 cm) cakes or one 10 ×3-in. (25.4 ×7.6 cm) cake*

BAKING TIME: *40 to 45 minutes for 8-in. (20.3 cm) cake pans, 60 to 70 minutes for a 10-in. (25.4 cm) cake pan*

8 oz (227 g) unsalted butter, softened

1 lb (454 g) granulated sugar

2.7 oz (77 g) Lemon Curd (page 231)

2 Tbsp (30 ml or 28 g) fresh lemon juice

Grated zest of 3 lemons

12 ounces (240 g) cake flour

1 Tbsp (12 g) baking powder

½ tsp (2.5 g) salt

8 oz (227 g) shredded coconut

5 large eggs

8 fl oz (237 ml or 227 g) whole milk

2 tsp (10 ml) vanilla extract

Preheat the oven to 350°F (177°C). Vegetable-spray and parchment-line the cake pans.

Cream together the butter, sugar, lemon curd, lemon juice, and zest for 5 minutes. Stop and scrape the bowl. Cream the mixture for another minute.

Sift together the cake flour, baking powder, and salt. Stir in the shredded coconut. Set aside. In a separate bowl, whisk together the eggs, milk, and vanilla.

Add the flour mixture and the milk/egg mixture alternately to the creamed butter mixture in three increments. Mix until the batter is smooth.

Pour the batter into the prepared pans and bake until a toothpick inserted in the center comes out clean.

NOTE: This recipe may be multiplied several times.

decorator's buttercream icing

EQUIPMENT: *5- or 6-quart mixer*

YIELD: *5 lb (2.3 kg)*

1 lb (454 g) unsalted butter

8 oz (230 g) white vegetable or hi-ratio shortening

1½ tsp (7.5 ml) lemon, vanilla, or almond extract

1 tsp (5 g) salt

3 lb (1.36 kg) confectioners' sugar

3 Tbsp (24 g) meringue powder

4½ fl oz (134 ml or 128 g) water, milk, heavy cream, or clear liqueur

Cream the butter and shortening with the paddle attachment for 3 minutes on medium-high speed. Stop and scrape the bowl. Cream for another minute. Add the flavoring and salt and mix until combined. Gradually add the sugar, then the meringue powder. The mixture will appear dry.

Add the liquid of your choice and beat until light and fluffy, 5 to 8 minutes. Keep the bowl covered with a damp cloth or plastic wrap.

Store the icing in an airtight container for 2 weeks in the fridge or freeze for up to 3 months.

NOTE: This recipe may be multiplied several times.

french vanilla buttercream

EQUIPMENT: *5- or 6-quart mixer*

YIELD: *2½ to 3 lb (1.1 to 1.4 kg)*

12 oz (340 g) granulated sugar

6 fl oz (177 ml or 170 g) whole milk

1½ Tbsp (⅜ oz or 10.6 g) all-purpose flour

¼ tsp (1.25 g) salt

1 Tbsp (15 ml) pure vanilla extract

1¼ lb (568 g) unsalted butter, cut up

3 fl oz (89 ml or 85 g) heavy cream

Make a custard by heating the sugar and milk in a double boiler over simmering water until the sugar crystals dissolve. Remove from the heat, add the flour, salt, and vanilla, and whisk until the flour is incorporated. Place over an ice bath until the custard has cooled slightly.

Pour the custard mixture into a mixer bowl. Add the cut-up butter and heavy cream and mix with the paddle attachment on low speed to fully incorporate the ingredients, or until the mixture starts to thicken.

Mix on the next-higher speed until the mixture starts to look light and fluffy. This can take 7 to 10 minutes or longer if making larger batches.

Store the buttercream in an airtight container for 2 weeks in the fridge or freeze for up to 3 months.

NOTE: If the buttercream curdles, it will just take a longer time for the butter to warm up. Continue beating until the butter softens and the mixture looks light and fluffy.

NOTE: This recipe may be multiplied several times.

swiss meringue buttercream

EQUIPMENT: *5- or 6-quart mixer*

YIELD: *2½ qt (2.4 l)*

12 oz (340 g) egg whites

1½ lb (680 g) granulated sugar

3 lb (1.36 kg) unsalted butter

2 Tbsp (30 ml) lemon, almond, vanilla, or orange extract or up to 3 fl oz (89 ml or 85 g) light rum, framboise, Kirsch, amaretto, or poire William

Lightly whisk the egg whites and sugar together over simmering water until the mixture is hot to the touch or a candy thermometer reads 140°F (60°C).

Pour the hot whites into a room-temperature bowl and whip with the wire whisk attachment on medium-high speed until doubled in volume. When the mixer stops, the meringue should not move around in the bowl. Meanwhile, cut up the butter into medium-size pieces (the butter should be slightly moist on the outside but cold inside).

Remove the whisk and attach the paddle. Divide the butter into four parts. Add the first part and mix on stir speed for 15 seconds. Then add the second part and mix on slow speed for 15 seconds, followed by the third and fourth parts. Slowly raise the speed of the mixer, starting with the lowest speed and raising the speed every 10 seconds until you reach medium-high.

Continue beating until the mixture begins to look light and fluffy. Stop the mixer and scrape the bowl. Reduce the speed to low. Add the flavoring and continue to beat on low speed for 45 seconds. Then beat on medium-high speed for 45 to 60 seconds.

Store the buttercream in an airtight container for 1 week in the fridge or freeze for up to 3 months.

NOTE: In hot weather, you can replace some of the butter with high-ratio shortening. High-ratio shortening is emulsified and contains water. It is not as greasy as commercial brands and does not leave an aftertaste on the back of your palate. High-ratio shortening can be substituted in any recipe that calls for butter or margarine. Popular brands are Sweetex and Alpine.

NOTE: This recipe may be multiplied several times.

amaretto mocha buttercream

EQUIPMENT: *5- or 6-quart mixer*

YIELD: *2½ qt (2.4 l)*

1 recipe unflavored Swiss Meringue Buttercream (preceding recipe)

4 Tbsp (60 ml or 15 g) instant espresso coffee

3 oz (89 ml or 85 g) amaretto

Put the buttercream into a mixer bowl and fit the mixer with the paddle attachment. In a separate small bowl, thoroughly mix the coffee and amaretto until the coffee is dissolved.

Slowly pour the coffee mixture into the buttercream. Beat with the paddle attachment on medium-high speed for 2 to 3 minutes to fully incorporate coffee mixture. Store the buttercream in an airtight container for 1 week in the fridge or freeze for up to 3 months.

NOTE: For Chocolate Mocha, replace the amaretto with Godiva Liqueur. For Praline Mocha, add 3 oz (85 g) praline paste.

NOTE: This recipe may be multiplied several times.

white chocolate buttercream

EQUIPMENT: *5- or 6-quart mixer*

YIELD: *3 qt (2.8 l)*

1 recipe unflavored Swiss Meringue Buttercream (page 208)

1 lb (454 g) white chocolate Ganache (recipe follows), refrigerated until slightly firm

4 fl oz (114 g or 118 ml) Godiva White Chocolate Liqueur

Put the buttercream into a mixer bowl and fit the mixer with the paddle attachment. With the mixer set on stir speed, add the white chocolate ganache, 4 oz (114 g) at a time, to the buttercream until all of it is incorporated.

Slowly add the Godiva liqueur. Beat until the icing is light and fluffy. Store the buttercream in an airtight container for 1 week or freeze for up to 3 months.

NOTE: This recipe may be multiplied several times.

ganache

YIELD: *1.75 lb (794 g)*

12 fl oz (355 ml or 340 g) heavy cream

1 lb (454 g) semisweet, bittersweet, or white chocolate

In a heavy saucepan, boil the heavy cream. Turn off the heat. Add chopped chocolate pieces or chocolate disks and let it rest until melted. Use a rubber spatula to stir the mixture until all the pieces are melted.

Pour the chocolate mixture into a room-temperature bowl and cover with plastic wrap. Let rest at room temperature if semisweet or bittersweet until the chocolate firms. Refrigerate the ganache until firm if white chocolate. White ganache will last for up to 2 weeks in the fridge. Dark ganache will last for several weeks in a cool dry kitchen.

NOTE: This recipe may be multiplied several times.

dark chocolate buttercream icing

EQUIPMENT: *5- or 6-quart mixer*

YIELD: *2½ to 3 qt (2.3 to 2.8 l)*

1 lb (454 g) unsalted butter at room temperature

4 oz (115 g) white vegetable or hi-ratio shortening

3 lb (1.36 kg) confectioners' sugar

4 oz (114 g) Dutch process cocoa powder

3 Tbsp (24 g) meringue powder

1 tsp (5 g) salt

2 Tbsp (30 ml or 57 g) whole milk

1 Tbsp (15 ml) vanilla extract

5 fl oz (150 ml or 140 g) chocolate liqueur

1 lb (454 g) semisweet or bittersweet chocolate Ganache (preceding recipe), left at room temperature to firm up

Cream the butter and shortening for 2 minutes. Stop to scrape the bowl. Cream the mixture for another minute.

Sift the confectioners' sugar and cocoa powder together. Add the sugar mixture, 1 cup at a time, to the creamed butter and shortening. Mix until well blended. Add the meringue powder and salt and beat for 1 minute. The mixture will appear dry.

Add the milk, vanilla, and chocolate liqueur to the buttercream. Beat until well combined.

Add the ganache, 1 cup at a time, and beat until light and fluffy. Store the icing in an airtight container for 2 weeks in the fridge or freeze for up to 3 months.

NOTE: This recipe may be doubled.

italian meringue buttercream

EQUIPMENT: *5- or 6-quart mixer*

YIELD: *2.18 lb (1 kg)*

1 lb (454 g) granulated sugar

8 fl oz (237 ml or 227 g) cold water

6 oz (170 g) egg whites (6 to 7 large egg whites)

1 lb (454 g) unsalted butter at room temperature

1 Tbsp (15 ml) vanilla extract

Bring the sugar and water to a boil in a medium-size pot. Clean down the sides of the pot with a pastry brush dipped in cold water to prevent crystallization of the sugar. When the sugar syrup comes to a boil, place a candy thermometer in the syrup.

When the temperature reaches 215°F (102°C), begin to whisk the egg whites on high speed for 5 minutes, until they form stiff peaks. Meanwhile, check the sugar syrup.

When the temperature reaches 238° to 240°F (114.5° to 116°C, soft-ball stage), remove the pot from the heat. Slowly pour the syrup in steady stream down the side of the bowl while the whites are still whisking. Make sure the syrup doesn't touch the wire whisk.

Continue whisking until the meringue completely cools down. This could take 6 to 10 minutes.

Add the butter, a piece at a time, while the mixer is still whisking. Add the vanilla and beat until light and fluffy.

If the buttercream gets too soft, refrigerate for 15 to 20 minutes and rebeat until it begins to look light and fluffy. Store the buttercream in an airtight container for 1 week in the fridge or freeze for up to 3 months.

NOTE: This recipe may be multiplied several times.

meringue icing

EQUIPMENT: *5- or 6-quart mixer*

YIELD: *2½ to 3 lb (1.1 to 1.4 kg)*

6 fl oz (180 ml or 170 g) water

1½ lb (680 g) plus 2 Tbsp (30 g) granulated sugar

8 extra-large egg whites

2 tsp (10 ml) Dominican, Bourbon, or Madagascar vanilla extract

Heat the water and sugar in a medium-size pot. When the sugar begins to boil, start beating the egg whites. Stop, add the 2 tablespoons (30 g) of sugar to the egg whites, and continue to beat. Beat until medium to stiff (but not too dry).

When large bubbles begin to appear in the syrup (approximately 240°F[116°C]), remove the syrup from the stove. Slowly pour the hot syrup into the bowl in a steady stream while the egg whites are still beating. Add the vanilla. Beat for 2 to 3 more minutes, until fluffy and glossy. Store the icing in an airtight container for up to 5 days in the fridge.

NOTE: This recipe may be doubled.

cream cheese buttercream

EQUIPMENT: *5- or 6-quart mixer*

YIELD: *1¼ qt (1.2 l)*

8 oz (227 g) unsalted butter

4 oz (114 g) white vegetable or hi-ratio shortening

10 oz (283 g) cream cheese (regular or mascarpone)

1½ lb (680 g) confectioners' sugar

1 Tbsp (8 g) meringue powder

2 Tbsp (30 ml or 28 g) heavy cream

1 tsp (5 ml) vanilla extract

1 Tbsp (15 ml) fresh lemon juice

Cream the butter, shortening, and cream cheese together for 3 minutes. Stop and scrape the bowl. Cream for another minute.

Slowly add the sugar to the cream mixture. Add the meringue powder, heavy cream, vanilla, and lemon juice. Beat for 1 minute on low speed to incorporate the ingredients and then beat on medium-high speed for 3 minutes.

Stop and scrape the bowl and then beat for 2 more minutes. Don't overbeat as the buttercream will become too soft for icing and piping.

Store the buttercream in an airtight container for 1 week in the fridge or freeze for up to 2 months.

NOTE: This recipe may be multiplied several times.

confectioners' glaze (gum glue)

YIELD: *6 oz (170 g)*

6 fl oz (177 ml or 170 g) water

2 Tbsp (24 g) gum arabic

Small bottle with lid

Measure the water and add the gum arabic in a small bottle with a lid. Shake vigorously for 30 seconds. Let the formula sit for 30 minutes and then shake vigorously again.

Keep in the refrigerator as the glaze develops a sour smell if left out at room temperature for more than 1 day.

NOTE: Use this on show pieces that require a high sheen.

quick glaze

YIELD: *6 oz (170 g)*

3 fl oz (89 ml or 85 g) water

3 fl oz (89 ml or 128 g) light corn syrup

Small container with lid

Measure the water and corn syrup and place in a small pot. Heat until the corn syrup dissolves. Let cool and place in a small container with lid.

Keep at room temperature. Will last for several weeks.

NOTE: Corn syrup and molasses are heavier than thinner liquids like water, milk, and juice. Instead of measuring roughly the same number of ounces in volume and weight, the weight will be 1 ½ times the volume. Thus, 4 fl oz (118 ml) of corn syrup will weigh not 4 oz (114 g) but 6 oz (168 g).

marzipan

EQUIPMENT: *5- or 6-quart mixer*

YIELD: *2 lb (907 g)*

1 lb (454 g) almond paste

1 lb (454 g) confectioners' sugar, plus a little more if needed

1 tsp (5 ml) vanilla extract

1 tsp (5 ml) light rum

3 fl oz (89 ml or 126 g) light corn syrup

Cut up the almond paste with a bench scraper and place in a mixer bowl. Attach the paddle and mix on low speed until some of the oil is extracted from the paste (about 30 seconds).

Add ½ lb (227 g) of the sugar and continue to mix while slowly pouring in the vanilla, rum, and corn syrup. Mix until the dough comes together and sticks to the paddle. Remove the paste from the paddle.

Sift the remaining sugar onto the countertop. Turn the dough out onto the sugar and knead in all of the sugar. If the dough is still sticky, knead in a little extra sugar. Knead until the marzipan has a fine, smooth texture. The mixture should feel soft but firm.

Double-wrap in plastic wrap and store in the refrigerator until ready to use. Will keep in the fridge for several months.

NOTE: Corn syrup and molasses are heavier than thinner liquids like water, milk, and juice. Instead of measuring roughly the same number of ounces in volume and weight, the weight will be 1 ½ times the volume. Thus, 3 fl oz (89 ml) of corn syrup will weigh not 3 oz (85 g) but 4½ oz (126 g).

NOTE: This recipe may be multiplied several times.

marzipan-fondant paste

YIELD: *3 lb (1.4 kg)*

2 lb (907 g) Marzipan (preceding recipe)

1 lb (454 g) commercial rolled fondant

Knead both pastes together. If the paste is sticky, knead in a little confectioners' sugar. Wrap in plastic wrap and keep in the refrigerator until ready to use. Will last for several weeks in the fridge.

Use this paste when you want a little more flexibility and strength in your marzipan.

NOTE: This recipe may be multiplied several times.

marzipan–chocolate fondant paste

YIELD: *3 lb (1.4 kg)*

1½ lb (680 g) Marzipan (page 218)

1½ lb (680 g) Chocolate Rolled Fondant (recipe follows)

Knead both pastes together. If the paste is sticky, knead in a little white vegetable shortening. Wrap in plastic wrap and keep in the refrigerator until ready to use. Will last in the fridge for several weeks.

NOTE: This recipe may be multiplied several times.

chocolate rolled fondant

YIELD: *1 ½ lb (680 g)*

1 ½ lb (680 g) commercial white rolled fondant

6 Tbsp (48 g) Dutch process cocoa powder

1 ¼ Tbsp (20 g) white vegetable shortening

1 tsp (5 ml or 2 g) Vermeer Dutch Chocolate Cream Liqueur or Godiva Liqueur

Knead the fondant until pliable. Make a well in the center and place 2 Tbsp (16 g) of the cocoa powder in it. Measure out 1 tsp (5 g) of the shortening and rub it in your hands lightly. Knead the shortening into the fondant and cocoa powder until the cocoa powder is evenly distributed.

Make another well in the center of the fondant and add another 2 Tbsp (16 g) of the cocoa powder. Measure out another 1 tsp (5 g) of the shortening and repeat the process of kneading the cocoa powder and shortening into the fondant. Repeat this a third time, using the remaining cocoa powder and another tsp (5 g) of the shortening. Knead until the cocoa powder and shortening are evenly distributed.

Make a fourth well in the center of the fondant. This time, add the liqueur. Rub the balance of the shortening into your hands. Knead it and the liqueur into the fondant until smooth and pliable. Wrap in plastic wrap and store in an airtight container at room temperature for up to several weeks until ready to use.

NOTE: This recipe may be doubled.

modeling chocolate, aka chocolate plastic

YIELD: *Approximately 1 ½ lb (680 g)*

DARK MODELING CHOCOLATE

1 lb (454 g) semisweet or bittersweet chocolate

5 fl oz (148 ml or 210 g) light corn syrup

WHITE MODELING CHOCOLATE

1 lb (454 g) white chocolate

4 fl oz (118 ml or 168 g) corn syrup

Finely chop the chocolate and place it in a bowl over simmering water. Stir to melt the chocolate evenly. Remove the chocolate from the water when three-quarters melted and stir until all the pieces have melted. Stir in all the corn syrup with a rubber spatula at once. Continue to stir until the chocolate starts to leave the sides of the bowl. For dark chocolate, this takes about 60 seconds. For white or milk chocolate, the process takes about 20 to 30 seconds.

Scrape the chocolate mixture onto a piece of plastic wrap. Spread out the chocolate about ¼ to ½ in. (6 mm to 1.3 cm) thick. Place another piece of plastic wrap on top of the chocolate. Refrigerate or rest in a cool, dry place to age for 24 hours.

Once aged, cut the chocolate plastic into smaller pieces and microwave pieces for a few seconds just to take the hard edge off the chocolate. Knead thoroughly with the heel of your hands until the chocolate has elasticity and a shiny coat. Wrap in plastic wrap until ready to use. Will last for several weeks in a cool dry room.

NOTE: Corn syrup and molasses are heavier than thinner liquids like water, milk, and juice. Instead of measuring roughly the same number of ounces in volume and weight, the weight will be 1½ times the volume. Thus, 4 fl oz (118 ml) of corn syrup will weigh not 4 oz (114 g) but 6 oz (168 g).

NOTE: This recipe may be doubled or tripled.

white modeling chocolate paste

YIELD: *1¼ lb (567 g)*

1 lb (454 g) white chocolate

4 oz (118 ml or 168 g) light corn syrup

Commercial rolled fondant (optional)

Newsprint paper

Cornstarch

Melt the chocolate in a double boiler over simmering water until two-thirds melted. Remove from the simmering water and stir until all of the pieces have melted.

Pour in the corn syrup all at once and immediately begin to stir the corn syrup with a rubber spatula. Continue to stir for about 30 seconds, until the chocolate thickens and looks slightly grainy. Don't overstir or you will ruin the chocolate.

Spread the chocolate on a piece of newsprint paper. The chocolate should be about ⅛ in. (3 mm) thick. Place in the refrigerator until firm, 2 to 4 hours.

Remove the chocolate from the paper. Wrap the chocolate in plastic wrap and refrigerate for 24 hours to complete the aging process. The next day, knead the chocolate with a little cornstarch until the chocolate is pliable.

NOTE: To color white chocolate, you must use oil-based colors. If you wish to use water-based colors, then you must add some commercial rolled fondant to the chocolate to temper the chocolate. In addition, if you wish the white chocolate to be more elastic or more manageable, adding the commercial rolled fondant will give you that.

First, weigh the chocolate. Add 2 parts white chocolate to 1 part commercial rolled fondant. Knead in as much cornstarch as needed to absorb the fat. Second, color the chocolate as desired and then wrap in plastic wrap and refrigerate for several hours before use. Otherwise, the chocolate will be much too soft to use.

NOTE: Corn syrup and molasses are heavier than thinner liquids like water, milk, and juice. Instead of measuring roughly the same number of ounces in volume and weight, the weight will be 1½ times the volume. Thus, 4 fl oz (118 ml) of corn syrup will weigh not 4 oz (114 g) but 6 oz (168 g).

NOTE: Newsprint paper is inexpensive paper that shoes and glassware are often packed with to absorb moisture. You can purchase this paper at any art supply store.

NOTE: This recipe may be doubled.

egg white royal icing

EQUIPMENT: *5- or 6-quart mixer*

YIELD: *1 lb (454 g)*

3 oz (85 g) fresh egg whites or pasteurized egg whites at room temperature

1 lb (454 g) confectioners' sugar, sifted

½ tsp (2.5 ml) lemon extract

Lightly whip the egg whites on medium speed using the paddle attachment until the whites are frothy (or form soft peaks). This takes about 3 minutes. Lower the speed and gradually add the sugar. Add the lemon extract and beat on medium-high speed for 5 to 8 minutes, or until the icing forms medium to stiff peaks. Cover the icing with plastic wrap and then store for up to 1 day in a glass container until ready to use.

NOTE: This recipe may be multiplied several times.

meringue powder royal icing

EQUIPMENT: *5- or 6-quart mixer*

YIELD: *1 ¼ lb (571 g)*

1⅜ oz (40 g) meringue powder

4 oz (118 ml or 114 g) cold water

1 lb (454 g) confectioner's sugar, sifted

½ tsp (2.5 ml) lemon extract

Add the meringue powder to cold water in a mixing bowl. Beat to soft peaks, about 3 minutes on medium-high speed. Slowly add the sugar.

Add the lemon extract and beat for 5 minutes on medium-high speed, or until the icing forms medium to stiff peaks. Cover with plastic wrap until ready to use.

The icing need not be refrigerated if kept in a cool dry place and used within 2 weeks. Rebeat before using.

NOTE: This recipe may be multiplied several times.

quick gumpaste

YIELD: *1 lb (454 g)*

1 lb (454 g) commercial rolled fondant

1 tsp (5 ml or 3 g) Tylose CMC

½ tsp (2.5 ml) white vegetable shortening

Knead the fondant until pliable. If the fondant is sticky, knead in a little cornstarch to prevent sticking.

Next, make a well in the center of the rolled fondant. Add the Tylose.

Rub the shortening into your palms and knead the paste for 3 to 5 minutes. Double-wrap the paste in plastic wrap and place in a zippered plastic bag or an airtight container. Let rest in the refrigerator (or a cool, dry place) until ready to use. This paste can be used immediately but will perform better if allowed to rest for 24 hours. Will last for months in the refrigerator.

NOTE: This recipe may be doubled but may be difficult to handle if tripled.

NOTE: Tylose can be replaced with 1½ to 2 tsp (7.5 to 10 ml) gum tragacanth, but the paste will need to rest for 12 to 24 hours before use.

flood icing

YIELD: *9 oz (255 g)*

½ to 1 oz (15 to 30 ml or 14 to 28 g) water or pasteurized egg whites

8 oz (227 g) Egg White Royal Icing or Meringue Powder (page 224 or 225)

Carefully stir the water or egg whites into the royal icing, a little at a time. After adding half the liquid, check to see if you have the right consistency. Continue to add the liquid until you have achieved a flow consistency. Add more liquid if necessary. Cover with plastic wrap to prevent drying.

HOW TO CHECK FOR FLOW CONSISTENCY

You have achieved a flow consistency if, after you draw a knife through the icing, the icing completely comes back together after you count to 10 seconds. If the icing comes together before 7 seconds, add a little more royal icing to thicken it. Check for consistency again. If the icing does not come together within 10 seconds, add a little more liquid.

Store the icing in an airtight container for up to 3 days in the fridge.

NOTE: This recipe may be doubled or tripled.

rolled fondant

YIELD: *2 lb (907 g)*

1 Tbsp (9 g) unflavored gelatin (1 envelope)

2 fl oz (60 ml or 57 g) cold water

1 tsp (5 ml) lemon, almond, or orange extract

4 fl oz (118 ml or 168 g) corn syrup

1 Tbsp (15 ml or 14 g) glycerin

2 lb (907 g) confectioners' sugar

½ tsp (2.5 g) white vegetable shortening

Sprinkle the gelatin over the cold water in a small bowl. Let it stand for 2 minutes to soften. Place it over a pan of simmering water until the gelatin dissolves, or use the microwave for 30 seconds on high. Do not overheat. Add the flavoring.

Add the corn syrup and glycerin and stir until the mixture is smooth and clear. Gently reheat if necessary or microwave for an additional 15 to 20 seconds on high. Stir again.

Sift 1½ lb (680 g) of the confectioners' sugar into a large bowl. Make a well in the sugar and pour in the liquid mixture. Stir with a wooden spoon. The mixture will become sticky.

Sift some of the remaining ½ lb (227 g) of sugar onto a smooth work surface and add as much of the remaining sugar as the mixture will take. Knead the fondant, adding more sugar, if necessary, to form a smooth, pliable mass. The fondant should be firm but soft.

Rub the shortening into your palms and knead it into the fondant to eliminate stickiness.

Wrap the fondant tightly in plastic wrap and then in a zippered plastic bag. Place it in the refrigerator for up to 2 months, until ready to use. Rolled fondant works best if allowed to rest for 24 hours.

NOTE: Corn syrup and molasses are heavier than thinner liquids like water, milk, and juice. Instead of measuring roughly the same number of ounces in volume and weight, the weight will be 1½ times the volume. Thus, 4 fl oz (118 ml) of corn syrup will weigh not 4 oz (114 g) but 6 oz (168 g).

NOTE: This recipe may be doubled.

pastillage

YIELD: 7½ oz (212 g)

7 oz (198 g) Egg White Royal Icing (page 224)

2 tsp (10 ml or 6 g) Tylose CMC

1 to 2 oz (28 to 57 g) cornstarch

Put the royal icing in a medium-size bowl. Make a well in the center of the icing and add the Tylose. Stir vigorously with a rubber spatula or wooden spoon. The icing will begin to tighten up and thicken.

Put the cornstarch on your work surface and dump the icing onto the cornstarch. Knead the icing into the starch until the paste becomes elastic and pliable. Wrap the paste in plastic wrap and place in a zippered plastic bag.

When ready to use, sprinkle a light coating of cornstarch on your work surface. Break off a piece of the paste and knead until there is no stickiness. Roll out the paste to the desired thickness and cut with cutters or an X-acto knife.

NOTE: This recipe may be doubled.

rolled fondant modeling paste

YIELD: *1 lb (454 g)*

12 oz (340 g) commercial rolled fondant

4 oz (114 g) Quick Gumpaste (page 226)

Knead both pastes together until pliable. If the paste gets sticky, sprinkle a little cornstarch on your work surface and knead into the paste. Double-wrap in plastic wrap and place in an airtight container until ready to use. Will last for 2 months in the fridge.

NOTE: This recipe may be double or tripled.

lemon, lime, or orange curd

YIELD: 2½ lb (1.1 kg)

8 large eggs (approximately 14 oz or 397 g)

2 egg yolks (approximately 1 oz)

1½ lb (680 g) granulated sugar

Grated zest of 10 lemons, limes, or medium-size oranges

Juice of 10 lemons, limes, or medium-size oranges (12 fl oz/355 ml or 340 g)

12 oz (340 g) unsalted butter, cut into ½-in. (1.3 cm) pieces

Beat the whole eggs, egg yolks, and sugar together in a stainless-steel bowl until well combined. Add the zest, juice, and butter.

Cook in a double boiler over simmering water, stirring constantly, until the curd starts to thicken, about 20 minutes. The curd is ready when it coats the back of a spoon. Strain immediately and cool over an ice bath.

Store the curd in a plastic container with plastic wrap placed directly on the surface of the curd to prevent a skin from forming. Then cover with a tight-fitting lid. Refrigerate until ready to use. Will last for 2 weeks in the fridge.

NOTE: More lemons, limes, or oranges may be needed to equal 12 fl oz (355 ml or 340 g). You could also use an unsweetened orange juice instead of squeezing the juice from the orange.

NOTE: This recipe may be doubled or tripled.

pineapple curd

YIELD: 2¾ lb (1.19 kg)

8 large eggs (approximately 14 oz or 397 g)

2 egg yolks (approximately 1 oz or 28 g)

1½ lb (680 g) granulated sugar

10 fl oz (296 ml or 283 g) unsweetened pineapple juice

4 oz (114 g) chopped pineapple, fresh or canned

2 fl oz (59 ml or 57 g) fresh lemon juice

12 oz (340 g) unsalted butter, cut into ½-in. (1.3 cm) pieces

Beat the whole eggs, egg yolks, and sugar together in a large stainless-steel bowl until well combined. Add the pineapple juice, chopped pineapple, lemon juice, and butter.

Cook in a double boiler over simmering water, stirring constantly, until the curd starts to thicken (about 15 to 20 minutes). The curd is ready when it coats the back of a spoon or resembles pudding in consistency.

Strain immediately and cool over an ice bath. Store in a plastic container with plastic wrap placed directly on the surface of the curd to prevent a skin from forming. Refrigerate until ready to use. Will last for 2 weeks in the fridge.

NOTE: This recipe may be double or tripled.

passion fruit curd

YIELD: *2¾ lb (1.19 kg)*

8 large eggs (approximately 14 oz or 397 g)

2 egg yolks (approximately 1 oz or 28 g)

1½ lb (680 g) granulated sugar

10 fl oz (296 ml or 283 g) frozen passion fruit juice drink concentrate, thawed

2 fl oz (59 ml or 57 g) fresh lemon juice

12 oz (340 g) unsalted butter, cut into ½-in. (1.3 cm) pieces

Beat the whole eggs, egg yolks, and sugar together in a large bowl until well combined. Add the passion fruit juice concentrate, lemon juice, and butter.

Cook in a double boiler over simmering water, stirring constantly, until the curd starts to thicken, 15 to 20 minutes. The curd is ready when it coats the back of a spoon or resembles pudding in consistency.

Strain immediately and cool over an ice bath. Store in a plastic container with plastic wrap placed directly on the surface of the curd to prevent a skin from forming. Refrigerate until ready to use. Will last for 2 weeks in the fridge.

NOTE: This recipe may be double or tripled.

sieved apricot jam

YIELD: *10 oz (283 g)*

8 oz (227 g) apricot preserves

4 fl oz (118 ml) cold water

Cook the preserves and water together until they begin to simmer. Strain and allow the mixture to cool. Place the jam in a jar with a tight-fitting lid. Refrigerate until ready to use.

NOTE: This recipe may be doubled or tripled.

pastry cream

YIELD: *1 lb (454 g)*

1 vanilla bean

10 fl oz (296 ml or 283 g) half-and-half

6 oz (170 g) granulated sugar

2 large eggs

1 large egg yolk

2 Tbsp (24 g) all-purpose flour

Split the vanilla bean lengthwise and scoop out the seeds. Place the seeds and the bean in a heavy saucepan with the half-and-half. Bring to a simmer and then strain to remove the seeds. Remove the vanilla bean.

In a separate bowl, whisk together the sugar, whole eggs, egg yolk, and flour. Gradually whisk in the hot half-and-half. Transfer back to the heavy saucepan. Whisk over medium heat until the mixture thickens and comes to a boil, about 5 minutes. Boil for about 1 minute.

Pour into a medium-size bowl and press plastic wrap directly on the surface of the pastry cream to prevent a skin from forming. Chill until cold. Will last for 3 days in the fridge.

NOTE: This recipe may be doubled or tripled.

FLAVOR COMBINATIONS

cake	filling	icing	rolled fondant
HI-YIELD YELLOW	Raspberry puree or Lime Curd	Swiss Meringue Buttercream	White or colored fondant with raspberry oil added
LEMON POUND	Lemon Curd	Italian Meringue Buttercream	White fondant
LEMON COCONUT	Lemon Curd	French Vanilla Buttercream	Rolled Fondant flavored with lemon extract
CHOCOLATE FUDGE	Ganache	Chocolate Buttercream	Chocolate Rolled Fondant
CHOCOLATE POUND	Creamy Peanut Butter	Amaretto Mocha Buttercream	Chocolate Rolled Fondant flavored with amaretto
RED VELVET	White Chocolate Ganache	Cream Cheese Buttercream	Colored fondant
CARROT*		Cream Cheese Buttercream	Colored fondant
PEANUT BUTTER	Creamy peanut butter or raspberry puree	White Chocolate Buttercream or Praline Mocha Buttercream	Colored fondant
DOMINICAN	Pineapple Curd	Meringue	White or colored fondant with pineapple extract
GERMAN CHOCOLATE	Ganache flavored with raspberry puree	Chocolate Buttercream	Chocolate Rolled Fondant
ALMOND WALNUT*		French Vanilla Buttercream	White or colored fondant
ALMOND PASTE	Raspberry puree	French Vanilla Buttercream	Colored fondant

These cakes are usually not split and filled.

afterword

In the end, only you can determine how successful you wish to become. Success as a cake artist can happen only with extremely hard work and a lot of dedication. There can be a lot of sleepless nights, especially when you're thinking about that huge order you perhaps should not have taken but took because you needed the cash flow. You may have days where you have only six cake orders so far for the next two weeks when you should have 20 or more and you're worried about the payroll; and other days where you got some local television or national coverage and suddenly you have 35 cake orders to fill within a few days!

When it rains, it pours, and when it's slow, it's dry-docking. It's sometimes hard to gauge work in the industry. For the most part, if it's slow for you, it's slow for your competitors. If you lease or rent your own space, this might be the time to start thinking about doing some private or semiprivate teaching to those who have an interest in your cake art. Students and prospective cake artists always want to take classes, and once you make a name for yourself you have the opportunity to expand your talents. Teaching during some nights when you know your business will be slow would be a great start.

You also need to have a great sense of humor if you wish to remain sane. You get out of it what you put into it. In the end, it's the art that keeps on giving, and for me, it's the art that keeps me smiling.

templates
and
cake-cutting
guides

TEMPLATES

These templates can be enlarged or reduced to fit the size of your cake.

Scalloped ovals, Textured Rose Cake

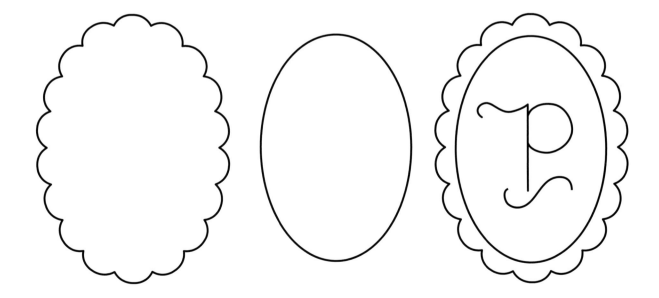

Scalloped ovals with initial, Textured Rose Cake

Large scalloped oval, Textured Ribbon and Rosebud Cake

Large scalloped oval (slightly wider), Textured Ribbon and Rosebud Cake

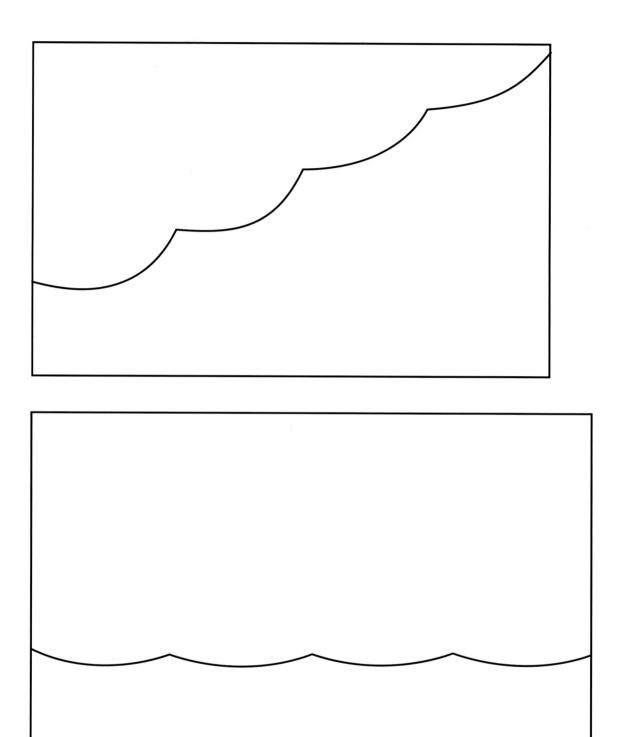

Scallop design left, Two-Tone Ribbon and Textured Leaf Spray Cake

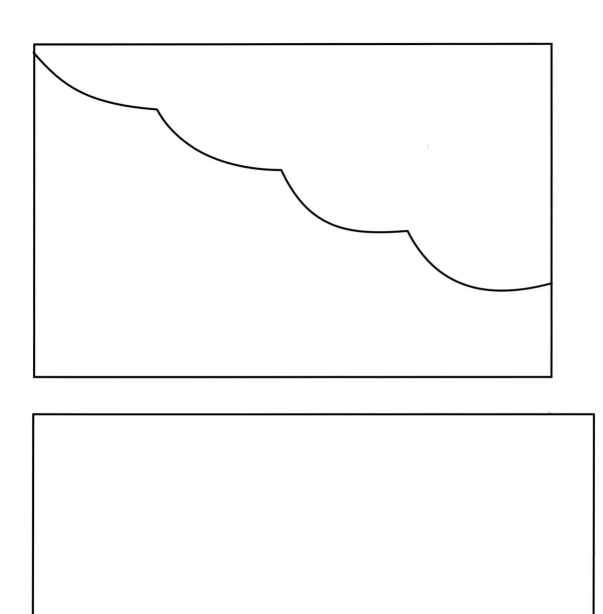

Scallop design right, Two-Tone Ribbon and Textured Leaf Spray Cake

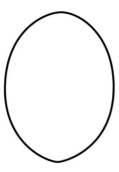

Closed tulip, Flooded Butterfly and Closed Tulip Cake

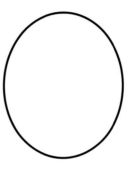

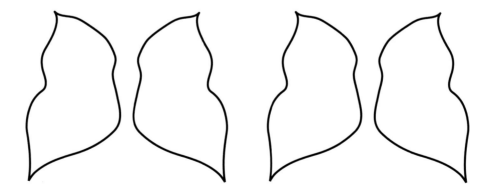

Butterfly and tulip, Flooded Butterfly and Closed Tulip Cake

Bells, Flooded Bell, Calla Lily, and Blue Tulle Cake

Hearts, Heart-Shaped Cake with Flooded Hearts and Carnations

Large heart, Heart-Shaped Cake with Flooded Hearts and Carnations

Monogram, Satin Stitch Monogrammed Cake

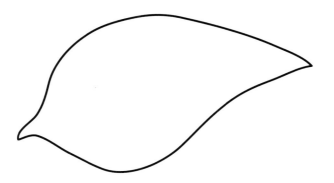

Leaf spray, Brush Embroidery Cake

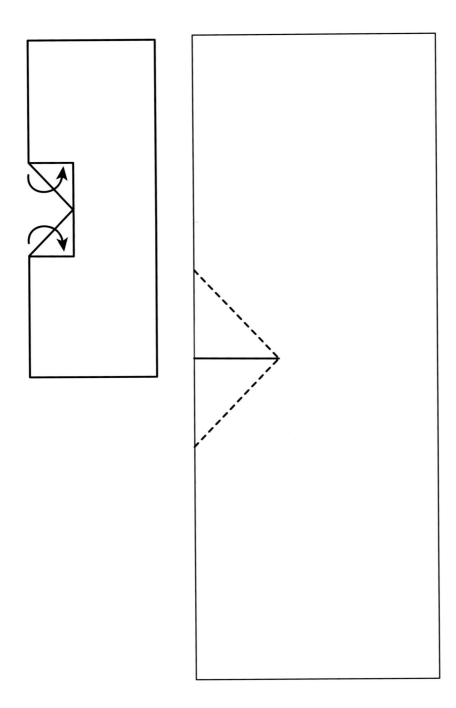

Tux 1, Groom's Cake

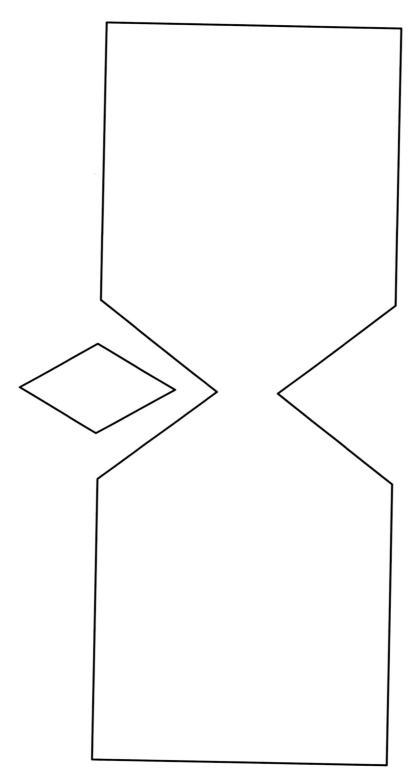

Tux 2, Groom's Cake

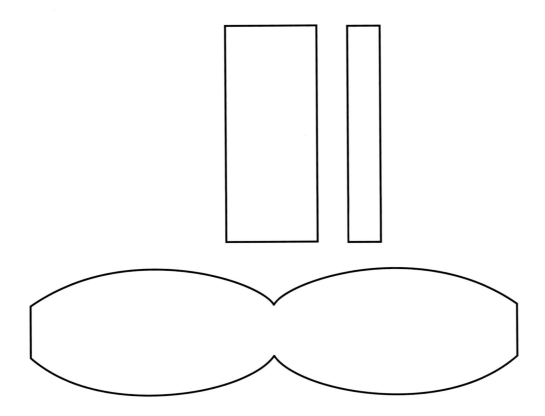

Bow tie, Groom's Cake

Triangles, Triangular Cake

Initials, Triangular Cake

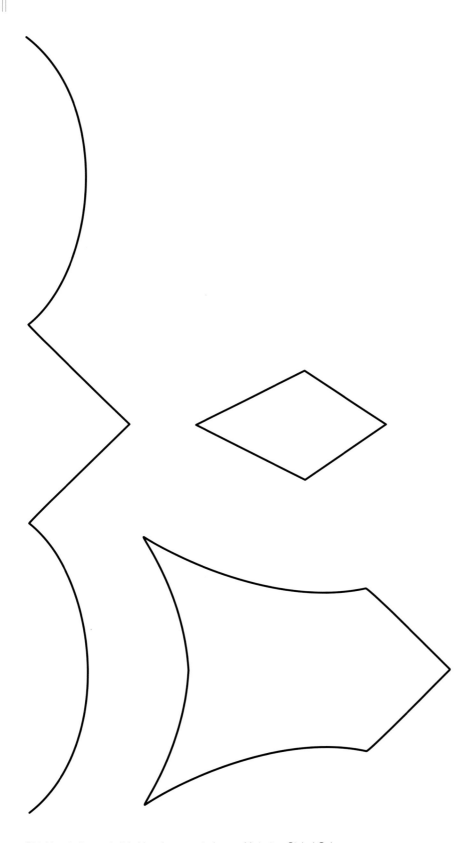

Shield and diamond disk, V and crescent shapes, Victorian-Styled Cake

Leaf motif, Victorian-Styled Cake

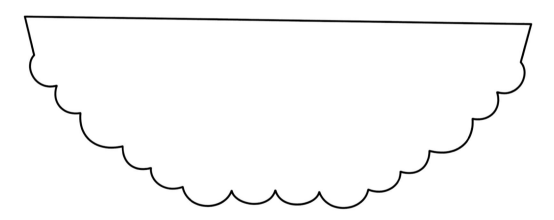

Shutters, Country Cottage Cake

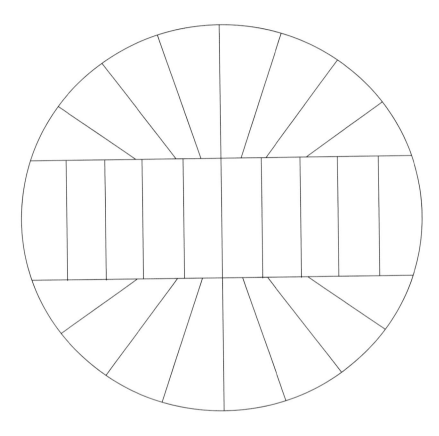

Round cake, 10 to 11 in. (25.4 to 27.9 cm)

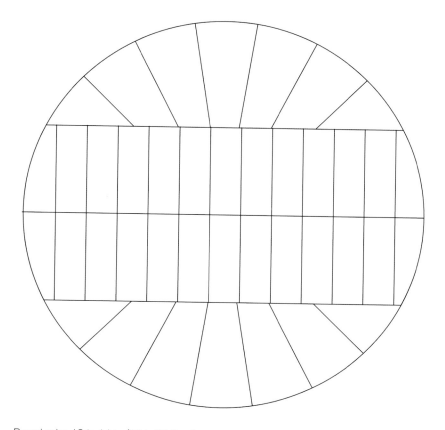

Round cake, 12 to 14 in. (30 to 35.6 cm)

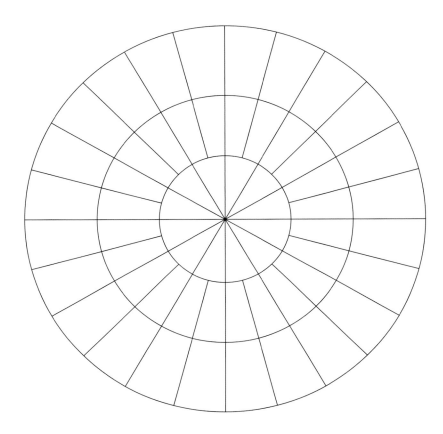

Round cake, 16 to 18 in. (40.6 to 45.7 cm)

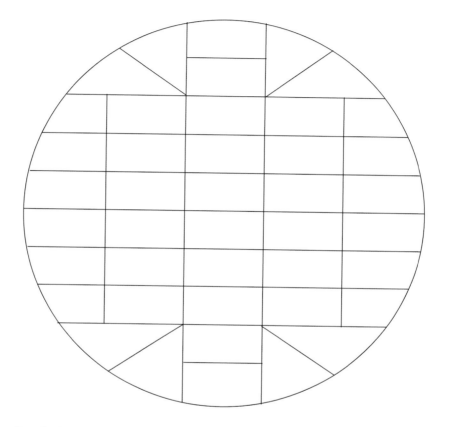

Round cake/square cuts

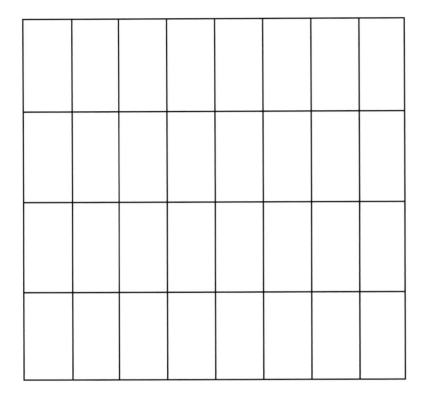

Square cake, 8 to 10 in. (20.3 to 25.4 cm)

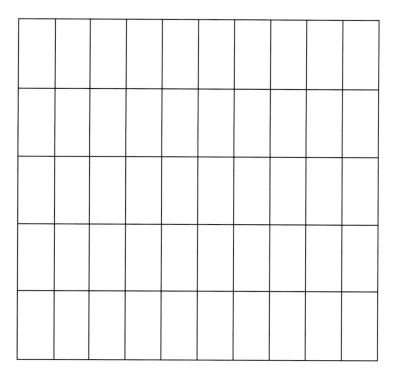

Square cake, 10 to 12 in. (25.4 to 30 cm)

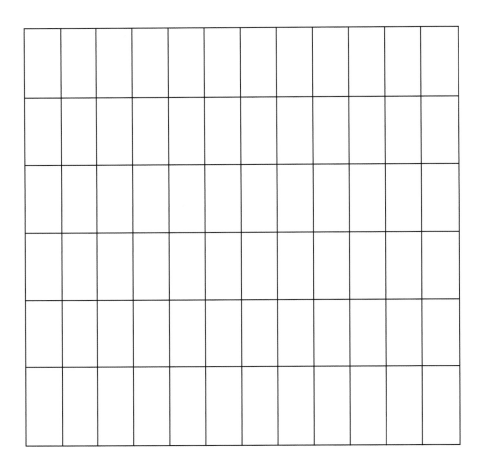

Square cake, 14 to 16 in. (35.6 to 40.6 cm)

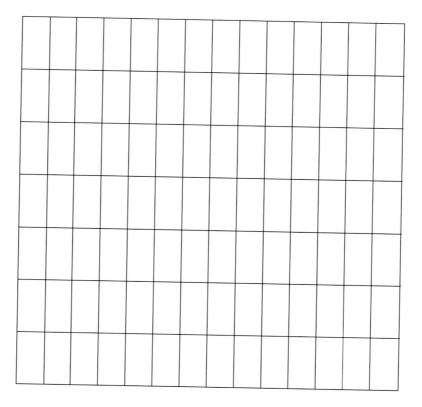

Square cake, 16 to 18 in. (40.6 to 45.7 cm), 98 servings

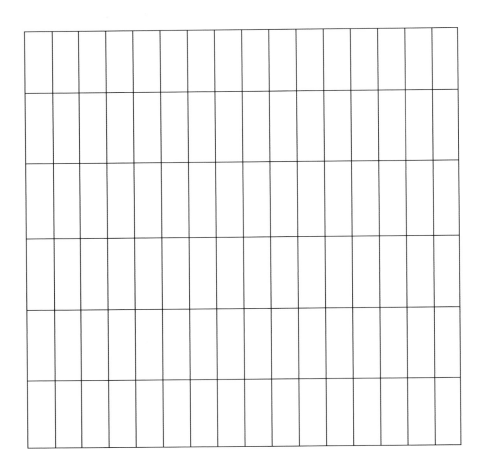

Square cake, 16 to 18 in. (40.6 to 45.7 cm), 96 servings

INDEX

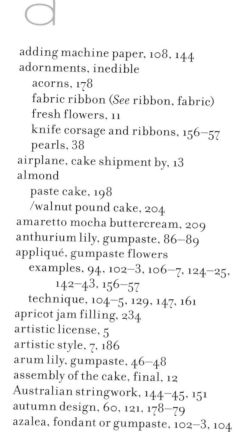

X-acto knife, 26, 32, 98, 105, 133, 180

yellow and white cake, 141, 142–47

Z

zoning laws, 184